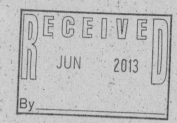

slow flowers

Four Seasons of Locally Grown Bouquets from the Garden, Meadow and Farm

slow flowers

Four Seasons of Locally Grown Bouquets from the Garden, Meadow and Farm

DEBRA PRINZING

author and co-creator of *The 50 Mile Bouquet*

PITTSBURGH

Slow Flowers
Four Seasons of Locally Grown Bouquets from the Garden, Meadow and Farm

Text and Images
Copyright © 2013 Debra Prinzing
www.debraprinzing.com

ISBN-13: 978-0-9832726-8-7

Library of Congress Control Number: 2012940820
CIP information available upon request

First Edition, 2013

St. Lynn's Press . POB 18680 . Pittsburgh, PA 15236
412.466.0790 . www.stlynnspress.com

Book design – Holly Rosborough
Editor – Catherine Dees
Horticultural Editor – Diane Szukovathy

Author Photographs © Mary Grace Long
Photo on page 61 © Ellen Spector Platt

Printed in Canada
on certified FSC recycled paper using soy-based inks

This title and all of St. Lynn's Press books may be purchased for educational, business, or sales promotional use. For information please write:
Special Markets Department . St. Lynn's Press . POB 18680 . Pittsburgh, PA 15236

10 9 8 7 6 5 4 3 2 1

To the flower farmers and florists of

the Seattle Wholesale Growers Market community,

especially to Kim Krajicek Millikin

and Nicole Monique Cordier,

whose friendship made my bouquet-making efforts

meaningful every week of the year.

TABLE OF CONTENTS

STOP, SMELL –
AND GATHER THE ROSES

My 52 Weeks of Local Flowers

One of the joys of gardening is to step out my back door and clip a few sprigs to bring inside. The day's prettiest blooms and just-unfurled leaves – gathered simply into a bunch and displayed in a jar of water – provide everything I need to start the day. The tiny arrangement graces my kitchen counter or brightens a spot by the keyboard, connecting me with the natural world even when I'm "stuck" indoors, away from my beloved garden.

Is this floral design?

I guess it is, but like avid gardeners everywhere, I certainly never considered myself a florist. After all, despite hundreds of hours of horticulture training, I never once studied the art of flowers, other than one weekend class on liturgical arrangements that I took with my Episcopal priest friend Britt Olson. Floral design was an entirely different sort of activity for which I wasn't qualified (I thought). I'm a writer and a lover of plants, but not an artist. I have written about floral design for years, interviewing top florists around the country for articles in magazines like *Seattle Bride*, *Romantic Homes* and *Sunset*. I loved reporting those stories, and I have to admit feeling a twinge of jealousy as I listened to flower artists answer questions about their style and technique, their use of botanicals and vessels – and especially, their inspiration.

I have spent my life observing and writing about creative people. But I didn't really believe that I was one of them! I was the classic journalist: a detached outsider documenting what she heard and saw.

Yet writers are sponges and driven by an insatiable, need-to-know curiosity. In pursuit of our stories, we can't help but absorb knowledge about myriad topics, taught to us by generous subjects whose own passion is infectious. That's exactly what happened to me while story-gathering for my most recent project, *The 50 Mile Bouquet*. I loved shaping the narrative about the many talented individuals who are part of the local flower movement.

During the creation of that book with photographer David Perry, my own bouquet-making activity was on the rise. I was beginning to see the gardens around me in a new way: in all four seasons, rather than only during July when the perennials peaked. The palette of possibilities expanded greatly, thanks to my interviews with the gifted flower farmers and designers profiled in *The 50 Mile Bouquet*.

My previously-spontaneous bouquet-making gestures soon became a weekly ritual. I discovered that just like designing a container garden or a display border, there is great satisfaction in choosing flowers and companion elements – and then assembling them into a beautiful composition in just the right vase.

I often photographed my design process. Documenting each step seemed like a good idea, either for my own reference, for a blog post or to illustrate a future lecture.

And then, one September day as I was making a bouquet out of burnished autumn leaves, green millet seed heads and the last dahlias of the fading summer, I had a brainstorm that led to the birth of this book, *Slow Flowers*. I jotted down some ideas, including this one:

> There's a common misconception that it's impossible, or at least tricky, to find enough
> beautiful ingredients in one's own garden or region during certain times of the year for
> creating interesting seasonal floral arrangements. Taking the Do-it-Yourself designer's point
> of view, I want to disprove that notion by making a bouquet-a-week – all year long. My goal
> is to inspire others to create personal bouquets with what's at hand, if only they begin to see
> what's around them with new eyes.

I launched the project then and there, and continued it for 52 weeks. As each season unfolded, so too did my passion for floral design. My experiment turned into a season-by-season, week-by-week book of ideas and inspiration for gardeners and DIY floral designers.

Why Slow Flowers?

The idea for the title of this book emerged organically. We had used the term "slow flowers" as part of the marketing for *The 50 Mile Bouquet* – and to our surprise, nearly every major newspaper and magazine that reviewed the book picked up on it as a reference to a cultural shift in consumer attitudes toward local, seasonal and sustainably-grown flowers.

So when editor Cathy Dees and publisher Paul Kelly and I got serious about finding a book title, *Slow Flowers* seemed like the "just-right" description of my one-year floral design experiment. Thanks to the culinary pioneers who popularized the Slow Food movement, it now seems like you can put "slow" in front of any term to convey a different philosophy or approach to that subject. When I say the phrase "slow flowers," there are those who immediately understand it to mean: I have made a conscious choice.

My blooms, buds, leaves and vines are definitely in season; not, for example, grown and brought in from elsewhere in the world during the wet, cold winter months in my hometown of Seattle. So, come December and January, my commitment to sourcing locally-grown floral materials sends me to the conifer boughs, colored twigs and berry-producing evergreens – and the occasional greenhouse-grown rose, lily or tulip, just to satisfy my hunger for a bloom.

Slow Flowers (the concept and the book) is also about the artisanal, anti-mass-market approach to celebrations, festivities and floral gifts of love. I value my local sources. If not clipped from my own shrubs or cutting garden, I want to know where the flowers and greenery were grown, and who grew them. Having a relationship with the grower who planted and nurtured each flower is nothing short of magical. I call so many flower farmers around the country my friends. They are the unsung heroes – the faces behind the flowers we love.

Finally, *Slow Flowers* reflects life lived in the slower lane. My family, friends and professional colleagues know that it's almost impossible for me to do anything slowly. I'm the queen of multitasking; I just can't help myself. There are too many exciting opportunities (or bright, shiny objects) that command my interest. But this "year in flowers" was altogether different. I can only compare it to the practice of praying or meditating. I didn't realize that those few hours I spent each week, gathering and choosing petals and stems, arranging them in a special vessel, and then figuring out where and how to capture the finished design through my camera lens, would be so personally enriching.

I used all my senses. Unplugged, away from electronic distractions, I studied the form, line, texture, subtle color and utter uniqueness of each stem. What a gift to slow down and experience the moment. I don't know much about *ikebana*, the Japanese art of arranging flowers, but I understand that silence and contemplation of nature are part of its practice. I experienced something similar. *Slow Flowers* forced me to work at a decidedly different pace as I embraced creativity, fearlessly.

I learned about my own preferences, design style and ability to look at the world of floral ingredients in an unconventional way. I learned that I really am a floral designer. Like me, you don't have to earn a certificate from the London School of Floral Design to create seasonally-inspired bouquets. You can find local blooms in your or your friend's garden, or from the fields, meadows and farm stands of local flower growers. Each bouquet tells a story about one moment in time, about Grandmother's cherished flower vase or the fleeting memory that returns with a whiff of lavender or lilac. That's one of the intangible gifts of bringing flowers into our lives.

I love the old-fashioned definition of a Florist, appropriately portrayed on a flower shop sign I noticed on a visit to Chicago: "One in the business of raising or selling flowers and ornamental plants." It underscores my belief that if you grow flowers and ornamental plants, you can also arrange them.

Gardeners are especially qualified in the art of floral design. After all, we have an intimate relationship with our plants, their bloom cycle, their natural form and character – and their seasonality. We also know what colors and textures we like when combined in the landscape. A vase can be a little garden, its contents gathered and arranged to please the eye.

So give it a try. Design a bouquet. Channel your inner floral designer and begin your own year with slow flowers.

...sweet flowers are slow...

William Shakespeare

SPRING

. . . And in green underwood and cover
Blossom by blossom the spring begins.

–Algernon Charles Swinburne

Just in time, spring arrives. The quiet, monochromatic days of winter are slowly nudged aside by bright, polychromatic blooms, fresh green foliage that seems to unfurl before your very eyes, and the wonderful smell of bare earth, ready to be cultivated. Thank goodness I planted spring-flowering tulip, daffodil and hyacinth bulbs last autumn!

This season, the floral designer's palette relies on pure and pastel hues, delicate flower forms and verdant fronds, blades and tendrils. Bouquet-making can be as simple as gathering a few stems in a bud vase – the perfect way to enliven a room and lift the spirit. Or they can be lush and full – an antidote to winter and a welcome to the gardener's season.

These organically-grown tulips and a few fragrant hyacinths are enough to take your breath away – delighting tourists and locals alike at Seattle's Pike Place Market. Gretchen Hoyt and Ben Craft of Alm Hill Gardens in Bellingham, Washington, raise the flowering bulbs in sheltering hoop houses, which help to warm the climate by a few degrees.

TULIPS & TWIGS

WHENEVER I BRING A TULIP BUNCH home from the grocery store or farmers' market, my first inclination is to drop them into a tall, clear glass vase. The art of arranging tulips couldn't be easier than that!

Then again, these primary-colored tulips call for something livelier than generic glass. My lime-green flea market urn is perfect; its color value is the same intensity as the flowers. My design challenge? Filling the vase's 6-inch-wide opening so my tulips remain upright rather than flopping over.

The solution: A dome-shaped flower frog. When placed in the base of the vessel, it is all that's needed to keep the flowers erect. The metal frog measures 4½ inches in diameter and is 2 inches high with ½-inch square openings.

To create this arrangement, I added all the red tulips first, cutting the stems short to draw attention to the egg-shaped flowers. Notice that the heights are slightly varied for interest. Vivid yellow tulips create a second tier, their longer stems and more slender flower heads hovering above.

Together, the tulips and the vase make a bold, graphic statement. The organic branches and twigs soften the design. Curly willow is placed irregularly, seeming to embrace the entire arrangement. As final touch, I added several camellia stems cut at different heights.

All you see are the plump, fuzzy buds, quite noticeable since I plucked off the glossy green leaves. The composition is now modern and stylish – anything but ordinary.

Ingredients:
    12 stems red tulips and 10 stems yellow tulips, grown by
      Alm Hill Gardens
    6 stems curly willow (*Salix matsudana* 'Tortuosa'), grown by Oregon
      Coastal Flowers
    8 stems *Camellia japonica*, from my garden

Vase:
    5-inch tall x 6-inch diameter matte green urn with handles

From the Farmer

Water lovers: Unlike most floral design ingredients, tulips and willow branches seem to keep growing in a vase of water. You'll notice that the tulip stems elongate a little each day. Some designers prefer to take the arrangement apart and re-cut the lengthened stems, but I like to observe the changes that occur. Willow is a water-loving plant, so you may discover that it sprouts tiny white roots under water and that small green leaves will push open, as if it is growing in soil. Enjoy a few days of this ever-changing dynamic.

ZEN IN BLOOM

THIS DESIGN TECHNIQUE ALLOWS YOU to showcase a single type of flower, with added interest from a sculptural twig framework. Fifteen just-picked daffodil stems fill a 6-inch cube vase. They are held in place by tightly-packed dogwood twigs that are lashed together with twine.

To make this design, start with a square or rectangular vase. Pour a layer of decorative pebbles into the bottom. Then line up several dozen twigs, cut to length so they completely cover the vase opening and rest on opposite edges of its rim. You may need sharp pruners to snip the twigs.

Secure the twigs with a loop of twine-wrapped wire, tied around the vase like a ribbon on a gift. Twine-wrapped wire is ideal for this step because it can be twisted taut and secure (you will need wire cutters to trim the pieces). Depending on the size of your vase, you will need to secure the twigs in two or three places.

Fill the vase with water before adding the flowers. Then insert the flower stems between the twigs, staggering their placement row by row. The tension holds the flowers erect. I used the classic trumpet-shaped daffodil, which was in bud when this arrangement was first made. Over the next several days, the flowers slowly opened, as if they were a living sculpture. There's a restful, Zen-like quality to this very simple floral presentation.

Ingredients:

15 stems common daffodils, from my garden

Multiple lengths of coral-pink twig dogwood, cut approximately 2 inches wider than the vase opening. Any straight, woody branch will work, including vine maple, pussy willow or the colorful twig dogwood (*Cornus sanguinea* or *C. sericea*)

Vase:

6-inch tall x 6-inch square glass vase (this design adapts to any square or rectangular glass vase)

Other supplies:

Decorative pebbles

Twine-wrapped wire (available at craft stores in natural or green)

Design 101

Borrow inspiration: The idea for this bouquet came from a project featured in *Design*, a publication of The Flower Arranging Study Group of the Garden Club of America. Whenever you're inspired by another designer's technique, it's important to give it your own twist rather than make a direct copy. For example, the original creation used florist's foam inside the container, but I found it unnecessary, especially since the pebbles and twigs are enough to hold the daffodil stems in place.

BEAUTY FROM BRANCHES

MY FRIEND LORENE EDWARDS FORKNER arrived for lunch holding a huge tangle of olive-green branches. "I pruned my *Kerria japonica*," she pronounced, not to show off her superior knowledge of botanical Latin nomenclature, but because this unusual shrub doesn't have a common name. The branches were bare when Lorene cut them, but having grown this plant myself in the past, I knew what was to come! I found a vase tall enough to hold the stems and also added some recently-cut branches from a flowering quince shrub.

After several days indoors near a sunny window, the wintry branches woke up. Their tiny buds opened into delicate flowers, giving me more than a week's worth of happiness. The *Kerria* is one of those unruly shrubs that can respond well to aggressive pruning. Its spring trimmings are an ideal floral element. The flowering quince grows much slower, but it will eventually require pruning, giving you more branches to force indoors.

As they open, I notice the similarity of the two different flowers. They resemble tiny rosebuds, which is not so surprising, since both *Kerria* and *Chaenomeles*, the quince, are in the *Rosaceae* plant family.

The buttercup-yellow buds and the dark coral flowers seem to dance together, supported by the wild-looking branches. Back-lit by the morning light, their dreamy quality takes my breath away.

Ingredients:
Kerria japonica 'Variegata', which has white-edge leaves
Flowering quince (*Chaenomeles* x *superba*), available in coral, red, pink or white

Vase:
17-inch tall x 7-inch diameter cream urn. This is my go-to vase for last-minute arrangements and it is tall enough to handle the branches, which are nearly three feet long.

From the Farmer

Jump-start spring: Many flowering shrubs and trees are suitable for indoor forcing. In addition to *Kerria* and quince, you can cut the bare branches of forsythia, witch hazel and numerous fruit trees. Harvest branches when their buds begin to swell, taking care to use proper pruning techniques. Re-cut the stems on a 45-degree angle and place them in a vase of clean water. Over time, the buds will respond to your home's warmer temperature and begin to flower. Be sure to change the water as you would with any floral arrangement.

CHOCOLATE-AND-VANILLA

WHENEVER I USE *Anthriscus sylvestris* 'Ravenswing' in a floral arrangement, it prompts the inevitable question: "What *is* that dark fern?"

An ornamental cousin of the herb chervil, Anthriscus is actually a purple-black perennial or biennial that's inclined to self-sow a little too aggressively in the garden (unless you remember to deadhead the dill-like flowers before they go to seed). As a sultry ingredient that contrasts beautifully with a white vase and white blooms, it's a favorite of mine.

The distinct leaves do have a fern-like appearance, and they lend a graphic pop to my white-footed dish and the fluffy white flowers from my friend Charlotte Behnke's *Viburnum tinus* hedge.

While this design could be top-heavy in such a shallow vessel, it works because I filled the square dish with a loosely formed piece of chicken wire. Shaped like a mushroom cap, the wire can be secured inside the vase with reusable florist clay or floral tape. It acts like a large, malleable flower frog to hold the woody branches and herbaceous stems in place.

Insert the chicken wire so the rounded top emerges a few inches above the rim of the container. Here, I placed the white flowers so they billowed out over the vase's edge. Next, I draped the dark *Anthriscus* foliage over each side of the square vase, tips pointing down. Two types of flowering branches give this arrangement some height: White-flowering bridal wreath spirea and dogwood with green button-like flowers. Together, these common garden ingredients make a sophisticated statement in chocolate and vanilla.

Ingredients:

8-11 *Viburnum tinus* blooms, harvested
from Charlotte Behnke's Seattle garden

6 stems *Anthriscus sylvestris* 'Ravenswing',
grown by Jello Mold Farm

6 stems bridal wreath spirea (*Spiraea
cantoniensis* 'Flore Pleno'), grown by
Charles Little & Co.

3 stems green dogwood (*Cornus* sp.),
harvested by Oregon Coastal Flowers

Vase:

6-inch square x 3-inch deep white ceramic
nut dish (overall height is 8 inches)

Design 101

Elevate for importance: There's something appealing about lifting a floral arrangement with a footed vase or dish. It's like giving your bouquet a little stage or platform to help it rise above its environment. This is especially noticeable with an arrangement designed to be viewed on all sides, such as a centerpiece. If you don't have a footed dish or urn, you can use a cake plate to elevate your flowers!

A FLORAL WELCOME

I RECEIVED THIS GLASS WALL VASE from my friend Jayme Jenkins, who owns an online garden emporium called Aha Modern Living.

"How would you use this?" she wrote, asking me to send her a photo of whatever I created. You may have seen similar pocket-style vessels that have a mounting hole and a flat back for easy hanging against a wall. They are usually planted with ferns or mosses to create a miniature terrarium.

But why couldn't this glass planting pocket double as a vase? Since my red front door already possessed a large screw for the holiday wreath, the location seemed tailor-made for a vase of spring flowers.

I paired several locally-grown garden hellebores (*Helleborus orientalis*) with dainty white snowflake flowers (*Leucojum aestivum*) picked from my garden. In order to corral the stems, I wound a length of curly willow into a loop and inserted it into the vase.

Then I cut the hellebores and snowflakes at varying lengths, arranging them in an asymmetrical display so that most of the flowers faced outward – towards anyone arriving on my front doorstep. Notice how the willow holds the stems upright and adds interest to the design.

Spring's cool outdoor temperatures helped extend the life of this arrangement. My only concern? Reminding the guys in my household to *gently* open and close the front door!

Ingredients:
- 10 stems garden hellebores (*Helleborus orientalis*), grown by Jello Mold Farm
- 12 stems summer snowflake (*Leucojum aestivum*), harvested from my garden
- 1 stem curly willow (*Salix matsudana* 'Tortuosa'), harvested by Oregon Coastal Flowers

Vase:
- 9-inch tall x 6-inch wide, teardrop-shaped wall vase (4-inch diameter opening)

Design 101

Just add white: There are some floral designers who abide by the "rule of white," which calls for adding white flowers to every design. Take a look at this arrangement and you'll notice that a few white blooms go a long way. The bell-shaped snowflakes are smaller than the plum-colored hellebores, but they add a lot of cheer to the design. Especially when viewed from a distance, white flowers are impactful, making any arrangement young and fresh-looking.

FRESH AND FRAGRANT

SPRINGTIME IS EMBODIED in this vase, isn't it?

You can almost smell the heady perfume associated with *Syringa vulgaris*, the common lilac. To me, the fragrance is associated with my lifelong relationship with flowers.

Here, I've played seasonal matchmaker, introducing bunches of purple, Oregon-grown lilacs to their lovely companions. Jadeite-green hellebores and fox grape fritillaries *(Fritillaria assyriaca)* are all that's needed to create a sublime bouquet for my fireplace mantel. The cream-colored pottery throws more attention to this eye-catching floral palette.

Using clean, well-sharpened pruners, cut each lilac branch at a 45-degree angle, stripping leaves that would be under water.

Arrange the flowers slightly asymmetrically, so their pendulous blooms drape farther over the left side of the vase. Next, gather small bunches of the green-hued hellebores and insert them as if they were a single stem. With this technique, smaller flowers have more impact. Finally, since the plum-and-yellow fritillary blooms are so delicate, add them like ribbons on a package, allowing them to naturally fall into place, cascading above and over the other flowers.

Ingredients:

10 stems purple lilacs (*Syringa vulgaris*), grown by Oregon Coastal Flowers
10 stems garden hellebores (*Helleborus orientalis*), grown by Jello Mold Farm
10 stems *Fritillaria assyriaca*, a spring-flowering bulb, grown by Choice Bulb Farms

Vase:

17-inch tall x 7-inch diameter cream urn

From the Farmer

Hellebore how-to: Anyone who grows hellebores in their garden knows how frustrating it is to cut a few blooms and bring them inside, only to watch them wilt in a vase of water. Now I enjoy success when I use hellebores in my bouquets, thanks to an important lesson shared by Diane Szukovathy, co-owner of Jello Mold Farm. "Harvest hellebores after they have matured past the flower stage and the seed pods are beginning to form," she advises. "By then, the petals have started to leather up and those hellebores will be rock solid in an arrangement for ten days."

JEWEL TONES

THIS INDIGO-BLUE VASE is a favorite of mine. It has beautiful surface details, including rows of raised, button-like dots that resemble embossing. When I tried to include it in a magazine photo shoot, however, the art director told me it competed with the flowers, so we couldn't use it. This time around, there's no one to say "no."

What says "yes" to this vase is the floral palette of fuchsia anemones, periwinkle bachelor's buttons *(Centaurea cyanus)*, a handful of plump white tulips and several snowy-white blooms from my mock orange shrub *(Philadelphus coronarius)*. These pure, cool-toned flowers hold their own against the vivid blue glaze.

To create the bouquet, I started by filling the vase opening with varying lengths of anemone stems. Notice how some of the flowers are upright, clustered near the center, while others spill over the rim. Next, I added the mock orange branches, cut from a shrub in my garden. At this time of the year, the flowers range from tiny, pearl-like buds to fully developed blooms resembling single-petal roses. The bonus? The white blooms are pleasantly scented, and they echo the soft form of the white tulips. The final touch of color comes from bachelor's buttons, which grow from a single stand in my garden. They are long-lasting when cut and the bloom has an attractive starburst form.

Ingredients:
12 stems fuchsia anemones (*Anemone coronaria* 'Galilee Pink), grown by Everyday Flowers
8 stems mock orange (*Philadelphus coronarius*), harvested from my garden
6 stems bachelor's buttons (*Centaurea cyanus*), harvested from my garden
7 stems white tulips, grown by Alm Hill Gardens

Vase:
8-inch tall x 6-inch diameter round vase with 5-inch opening

Design 101

Color wheel lesson: The flowers and vase combination illustrate an analogous color palette. Analogous colors are adjacent to one another on the color wheel (see page 132). Fuchsia, purple and indigo are pleasing when viewed together because they each share varying quantities of the primary color blue. White floral accents offset the black centers of the anemones, adding a graphic punch to this composition.

STILL LIFE WITH FLOWERS

TWO BUNCHES OF MY FAVORITE SPRING FLOWERS are all that's needed to fill this charming vintage vase. The pale mint pottery plays nicely with the ranunculus's green foliage, stems and buds. And a bit of green peeks out from the lilac tips. The joyous shades of apricot, coral and pink in the mixed bunch of ranunculus put a smile on my face.

Even though this vase is relatively small, its 5 x 5-inch opening accommodated one of my smaller vintage flower frogs, which anchors the lilac stems. I cut them fairly short, leaving only 3-4 inches of stem, which ensures that the white clusters drape gracefully over the rim of the vase.

The lilacs are snugly arranged, yet there's still plenty of space between their fragrant blossoms to accommodate the ranunculus. Grown from a tiny tuber, the ranunculus produces fern-like green foliage, fleshy stems and tightly packed round buds that open to reveal layer upon layer of soft, curved petals. Placed in a random pattern, with the stem lengths varied for interest, they convey the new, hopeful spirit of the season.

When photographing the arrangement, I played around with different display ideas. Here, a wooden wine crate doubles as a shadow box, while a green-stained Ikea planter (turned upside down) is the perfect pedestal. Together, they make an alluring stage for my floral still life.

Ingredients:
10 stems lilac (*Syringa vulgaris*), grown by Oregon Coastal Flowers
12 stems *Ranunculus asiaticus*, including 'La Belle' and 'Super Green' varieties, grown by Everyday Flowers

Vase:
5-inch tall x 5-inch wide x 3-inch deep vase (overall height is 5½ inches)

From the Farmer

Extending the vase life: For decades, it's been the conventional wisdom of florists that woody shrubs, such as lilacs and hydrangeas, benefit from a second cut, a vertical slice up the center of the stem, to increase the surface area that can absorb water. But according to professors Lane Greer and John M. Dole, authors of *Woody Cut Stems for Growers and Florists*, a research-based reference, the practice "has never been proven to extend vase life." The best thing you can do is to use clean, sharp pruners and refresh the vase water every day or so.

FIRST PEONIES OF THE SEASON

THE INTENSE RUBY-RED PALETTE IS SHARED by these ruffled peonies and my art glass vase. I love the interplay of the two textures, hard and soft in balance; so naturally, the other ingredients needed to feel lighter in color and texture. I chose two types of ornamental alliums – white and lavender – to join the peonies. Lady's mantle, a spring perennial, contributed leaves that look like pleated petticoats (green ones, that is).

This is one of those arrangements that you can make by hand like a bridal bouquet. Once all of the flower stems are in place, the entire bouquet can go right into a vase, forming a softly shaped dome.

I began grouping the peonies in my left hand, holding them gently between my thumb and forefinger. I made adjustments with my right hand, pulling out individual stems to create an overall rounded bouquet. Next, I added the purple alliums, inserting them in the gaps between the peonies until their stems also rested in my left hand. That way, each flower can be appreciated individually rather than as one mass of color.

Similarly, I threaded the white alliums into the bouquet. Once I was happy with this overall form, I added a "collar" of green lady's mantle foliage, which gives the bouquet its polish. Before placing the bouquet in my vase, I re-cut all the flower stems to a consistent length.

Ingredients:
10 stems red peonies, grown by Ojeda Farms
7 stems each 'Purple Sensation' and 'Cowanii' ornamental alliums, grown by Choice Bulb Farms
12 stems lady's mantle foliage (*Alchemilla mollis*), harvested from my garden

Vase:
9-inch tall x 5-inch diameter hand-blown glass vase

Design 101

Create a collar: You can use flowers or foliage to ring the base of a bouquet or arrangement as a finishing detail. This technique is usually done as the bouquet's last step. For this arrangement, I pre-cut the greenery and then added it beneath the peonies, slightly overlapping each stem as I worked around the circumference of the bouquet. Here, the lady's mantle visually separates the dark red peonies from the wine-red vase.

A SOFTER SIDE OF GREEN

THE IMPETUS FOR THIS BOUQUET took place during a spring visit to Peterkort Roses in Portland, Oregon. I couldn't take my eyes off their 'Supergreen' hybrid tea roses. A beautiful shade of pale chartreuse, with slightly ruffled petals, these uncommon roses drew me in and I knew I had to use them in a bouquet. Thankfully, Sandra and Norman, the sister-and-brother team who run the Peterkort family rose farm, sent me home with a luscious bunch to play with.

I gathered other soft, pale green botanicals to join the roses. The silvery end of the foliage spectrum includes lamb's ears and Dusty Miller, velvet to the touch and both quite easy to grow. Fluffy and delicate, the green-and-white variegated Star of Bethlehem surprised me as much as those chartreuse roses. Are they flowers? Are they greenery? I like that it's hard to tell.

I started the bouquet by arranging a layer of soft foliage, which acts as a natural "frog" for holding the other flower stems erect. Here, the Dusty Miller's deeply-cut leaves drape nicely over the edge of the basket and the lamb's ears are more upright. Once the foliage is in place, it's time to add the other ingredients. I stripped all the leaves from the roses and varied their stem lengths for a more naturalistic placement. Finally, several apricot spires of *Verbascum* added height, their tawny flowers echoing the natural rattan of my basket.

Ingredients:

15 stems Dusty Miller foliage (*Centaurea cineraria*), grown by Charles Little & Co.

5 stems lamb's ears (*Stachys byzantina*), grown by Charles Little & Co.

15 stems 'Supergreen' hybrid tea roses, grown by Peterkort Roses

9 stems Star of Bethlehem (*Ornithogalum nutans*), grown by Choice Bulb Farms

6 stems *Verbascum* 'Caribbean Crush', grown by Jello Mold Farm

Vase:

7½-inch tall x 7-inch diameter woven basket with a 6-inch tall x 6½ inch wide glass insert

Eco-technique

Vase in an instant: Any container can double as a flower vase as long as you can hide a watertight vessel inside of it. This simple, budget-conscious technique instantly expands your design choices. I frequently pick up glass vases for 50-cents to a few dollars at the thrift store, which means I always have extras on hand to tuck inside boxes, baskets, tins – and even leaky watering cans .

PITCHERS OF POPPIES

WHENEVER ICELAND POPPIES SHOW UP at the farm stand they are quickly snatched up. Why do we love them so? Perhaps it's because of their pure, vibrant petal colors with the charming button-like centers. Or it's their uncomplicated forms – they remind me a lot of the way I drew flowers as a child.

And then there are their buds, encased in a fuzzy shell that pops open to reveal the crinkled bright petals inside, ready to bloom.

Poppies need little competition to dazzle in the vase, so I chose only a few additional ingredients to fill my favorite pitchers. Since red and green are perfect complements on the color wheel, I thought the orange-red poppies would look beautiful in my old-fashioned mint-green pitcher. I added the blue-green *Cerinthe major*, an almost iridescent perennial that cascades over the container's rim. The delicate rattlesnake grass has a hazy effect, its tiny seed heads shimmering as if in a breezy meadow.

For the arrangement in my clear glass pitcher, I chose two types of variegated cream-and-green leaves to offset the egg-yolk-yellow poppies. The bold *Astrantia* foliage came from my garden, while the smaller leaves are from a variegated mint. These flowers gave me days of happiness, all the more enjoyable because they were a gift from the farmer who grew them.

Ingredients:

(Green pitcher)

10 stems coral-red Icelandic poppies (*Papaver nudicaule*), grown by Jello Mold Farm

6 stems *Cerinthe major* 'Purpurascens', grown by Jello Mold Farm

7 stems rattlesnake grass (*Briza media*), grown by Jello Mold Farm

(Glass pitcher)

10 stems bright yellow Icelandic poppies (*Papaver nudicaule*), grown by Jello Mold Farm

10 stems *Astrantia major* 'Sunningdale Variegated' foliage, harvested from my garden

7 stems golden apple mint (*Mentha* x *gracilis*), grown by Charles Little & Co.

Vase:

8-inch tall x 5½-inch wide glazed ceramic pitcher

9-inch tall x 5½-inch wide Mexican glass pitcher

From the Farmer

Poppy care: Many garden books recommend that you sear the cut tips of these poppies in a flame or submerge them in a beaker of boiling water in order to extend their vase life. It has been thought that the extreme heat will soften the tougher outer stem and increase the surface area for absorbing moisture in the vase. But in fact, according to Diane Szukovathy of Jello Mold Farm, the poppy's hairy stem collects more foreign matter that contributes to bacterial build-up in the vase than with smoother-stemmed flowers. Because of this, she says, "heating the stems 'cooks' them, making the flower more susceptible to colonization by bacteria." Diane's best tip: "Every few days, re-cut the stems and change the water."

JOYEUX ANNIVERSAIRE

I CREATED THIS BOUQUET as a birthday gift for my friend Carrie Krueger. The soft and feminine gathering of blooms, paired with a vintage butter-yellow Wedgwood Jasperware trumpet vase, makes a complete package. When you give a gift bouquet, it's nice to branch out from ordinary clear glass and choose a vessel that will be used again and again by the recipient.

I started with several ingredients I inherited when we moved into our new home. Witnessing the garden's first spring and summer seasons was a thrill, including the peonies' unfurling. I like using the same flower in various stages of growth, so here I added several marshmallow-soft buds to the one large open peony. Across the garden, a mauve-colored lilac beckoned from under the mature cherry tree. And nearby, a mound of bachelor's buttons provided the essential indigo-blue floral accents.

Next, I added ingredients grown by local flower farmers. The trio of unusual 'Supergreen' hybrid tea roses sparkles as companions to the peonies. Lustrous and velvety, the Dusty Miller and lamb's ears foliage provide subtle touches of silver-green. And the final accent is the Star of Bethlehem, with dainty bell-shaped, green-and-white variegated flowers.

Ingredients:

- 5 stems hot-pink peonies (variety unknown), harvested from my garden
- 5 stems late-blooming lilac (*Syringa* x *prestoniae*), harvested from my garden
- 5 stems bachelor's buttons (*Centaurea cyanus*), harvested from my garden
- 3 stems 'Supergreen' hybrid tea roses, grown by Peterkort Roses
- 6 stems each Dusty Miller (*Centaurea cineraria*) and lamb's ears (*Stachys byzantina*), grown by Charles Little & Co.
- 6 stems variegated Star of Bethlehem (*Ornithogalum nutans*), grown by Choice Bulb Farms

Vase:

9½ inch tall x 5⅞ inch diameter Wedgwood Jasperware trumpet vase

Design 101

Unity and variety: In design theory, "unity" and "variety" are interrelated principles. Unifying features tie a composition together; in this arrangement the silvery-green foliage suggests a sparkly embroidery thread embellishing a shawl. Variety lends interest to a design, eliminating the ordinary. Here, the pleasing mix of ingredients from the cooler side of the color wheel does the trick, with a range of floral hues from pale green and lavender to deep fuchsia and indigo.

A BIT OF PURPLE HEAVEN

WHEN MY FRIEND DEE NASH saw this bouquet she proclaimed "this is a bit of purple heaven!"

The wistful arrangement of blue, purple and plum flowers looks quite awesome against the chartreuse vase. It includes ingredients gathered on a weekend in early June when I traversed the state of Washington with Lorene Edwards Forkner, a friend and fellow writer. We left Seattle to drive to Pullman, where Suzanne St. Pierre and Scotty Thompson hosted us as speakers at Living in the Garden, one of the most charming country nurseries you'll ever find.

Suzanne sent us to visit Jane Stratton of Sunshine Crafts and Flowers on Old Moscow Road, just a few miles away. Jane's cut-flower farm and bouquet subscription service is a hit with her local customers and florists. We gazed across her orderly fields of perennials, annuals, ornamental shrubs and grasses, beauty bursting from every row. And then we began to snip our favorites!

On our drive home, the car was filled with plants, antiques and buckets of Jane's beautiful, Eastern Washington-grown flowers. I was delighted to combine them with several just-picked stems grown in the western part of the state. Together, this vase contains the floral bounty of the Pacific Northwest.

Ingredients:
5 stems dark purple lilacs (*Syringa vulgaris*), grown by Sunshine Crafts and Flowers
7 stems blue perennial bachelor buttons (*Centaurea cyanus*), grown by Sunshine Crafts and Flowers
7 stems reddish-pink 'Nora Barlow' columbine (*Aquilegia* hybrid), grown by Sunshine Crafts and Flowers
5 stems purple ornamental alliums, grown by Jello Mold Farm
20 stems burnet (*Sanguisorba menziesii*), grown by Jello Mold Farm

Vase:
11-inch tall x 5½-inch citron-green crackle glaze vase

Eco-technique

Traveling with flowers: I can't resist taking flowers with me or bringing them home. If it's a car trip, place flowers in a stable bucket with just a few inches of water to hydrate the stems (but avoid splashing). Store on the shady side of the car. If you're traveling by air, wrap the stems in wet paper, cover with a plastic bag and then wrap the entire bunch in kraft paper that extends above the blooms. As soon as you arrive at your destination, re-cut all the stems, place in fresh water and possibly a refrigerator. I've been known to use a hotel wastebasket and mini-bar fridge for this step!

SUMMER

In summer, the song sings itself.

–William Carlos Williams

C ome summer, the garden's splendor is irresistible. The long days of sunshine, the kiss of warm air and the unrestrained joy we feel when surrounded by all that grows and blooms… together these moments define summer's sweet spot.

The season presents an abundance of choice to gardeners and floral designers alike. Backyard beds and mixed borders explode in a brilliant, saturated floral color. Field flowers reveal botanical variety, fragrance and textures that please the senses. The savory and sweet flavors from herb gardens, berry patches and orchards symbolize summer. And it's entirely possible to do the same thing with the season's flora. Live in the moment and relish the fleeting beauty of a just-picked rose, dahlia or zinnia. To do so is a very special ritual – one we spent nine months of the year anticipating. Ahh, summer!

Dazzling dahlias embody summertime. I photographed this charming cactus-formed variety called 'Camano Sitka' at Corralitos Gardens near Santa Cruz, California, where Kevin Larkin and Karen Zydner raise both dahlia cuttings and seasonal cut flowers for a passionate following of customers.

A CERTAIN VINTAGE

I DISCOVERED THIS MOCHA-COLORED VASE with a chevron pattern on the shelf of Old Goat Farm, my friends Gary and Greg's country nursery in Orting, Washington. Greg was selling off his vintage collection of Royal Copley pottery and I couldn't resist the vase's neutral, mousy color. The inside appealed to me, too, as it was finished in a citron-yellow glaze. The oval form is uncommon, but a very useful shape for presenting flowers in a vase.

I've used this simple vessel for many floral demonstrations, mainly because its opening holds more stems than you'd think, adding up to a full, billowy arrangement.

It wasn't until I came home with a few bunches of reddish-maroon sweet William flowers that I noticed the rosy undertones in Greg's vase. This old-fashioned perennial and the 1940s vase feel just right together, sharing the same vintage. They remind me of something I would have seen on my grandmother's screened-in front porch in Indiana.

To create the design, I needed a unifying foliage element. The plush leaves from my garden's *Heuchera* 'Green Spice' are perfect here. Notice how the leaves' deep-wine veining picks up both the flower and vase tones. I cut the longest heuchera stems on the plant (about 4 inches). If you put enough of them inside the vase they will stay nicely in place. Next, I added the sweet William flowers, alternating brighter red flower heads with darker wine-colored ones. And finally (remember my rule of white?), I added several short branches from the mock orange shrub in my backyard. It, too, is one of those heirloom shrubs that you could find in grandmother's cutting garden.

Ingredients:

25 stems heuchera foliage (*Heuchera* 'Green Spice'),
   harvested from my garden

7 stems sweet William (*Dianthus barbatus* var. *nigrescens*
   'Sooty'), grown by J. Foss Garden Flowers

5 stems mock orange (*Philadelphus coronarius*),
   harvested from my garden

Vase:

6-inch tall 1940s vase with a 7-inch x 3-inch oval opening

Eco-technique

Just add foliage: Thanks to the eco-conscious designers I've met and interviewed, I am quite wary of using florist's foam, a formaldehyde-based product, to stabilize arrangements. Designing around a base of foliage offers a greener way to keep flower stems upright in a vase. Choose leaves that are large, fluffy or textured. Then, insert your other floral ingredients through this vegetation. For example, in this bouquet I placed the heuchera leaves first; then I added the sweet William and mock orange stems. Everything stays just where I want it.

SUMMER GLOW

WHEN YOUNG CHILDREN DRAW FLOWERS in a vase, they often choose bright crayon colors: fire engine red, sunny yellow, hot pink. That cheerful palette evokes one idea of a "summer bouquet," but as our taste and style evolves, so does our preference for subtle or uncommon colors. This soft arrangement in a copper flowerpot is one example. It captures the warm tones of coral, peach and terra cotta. Color experts describe this palette as "nurturing, energizing and welcoming."

This design began with the russet-brown foliage called 'Coppertina', a variety of the ninebark shrub. I selected all the other flowers to echo the dark leaves, including apricot-hued foxtail lilies, pale peach stock, apricot snapdragons and rosy-pink yarrow. I first gathered the stems in a clear glass vase, starting as I often do with the foliage, then adding the medium-sized flowers and finally, the tallest elements.

I loved the combination, but the vase left me wanting more. And then I remembered this unusual six-sided metal planter, a years-old gift from my husband Bruce. The bouquet seemed tailor-made for the glowing patina of aged copper. Photographed in our living room with the morning light dancing across petals and buds, the composition is not a garden-variety summer bouquet – it's a more sophisticated take on the season's floral gifts.

Ingredients:

- 20 stems ninebark (*Physocarpus opulifolius* 'Coppertina'), grown by Jello Mold Farm
- 11 stems pink yarrow (*Achillea millefolium*), grown by Jello Mold Farm
- 7 stems pale peach stock (*Matthiola incana*), grown by Everyday Flowers
- 5 stems apricot snapdragon (*Antirrhinum maius* 'Tangerine Trumpet'), grown by Everyday Flowers
- 5 stems foxtail lily (*Eremurus* x *issabellinus*), grown by Choice Bulb Farms

Vase:

- 7-inch tall x 7½-inch diameter copper planter with a 5½-inch opening

Design 101

Tonal color palettes: Sometimes called "monochromatic," a tonal theme incorporates different shades of colors in the same group. Here I used a combination of pale, medium-toned and dark floral elements in the pink-peach-copper color family. What makes the composition interesting (rather than plain) are the many uncommon shapes and textures. Try this technique with varying shades of gold, green, silver or burgundy – your bouquet will look modern and sophisticated.

A STROLL IN THE GARDEN

SOMETIMES THE BEST WAY to approach floral design is to start with the right vessel and allow its style and scale to guide your flower choices. My crackle-glazed celadon vase blends nicely with many botanical elements; thus I knew it would accommodate a tall, lavish arrangement built around the beautiful "double" Shasta daisies from the Southern California garden where I lived for several years, before returning to Seattle.

The morning I gathered these refreshing white and yellow ingredients, it was still cool and the sun wasn't yet beating down. As I walked through the garden, I snipped small quantities of flowers, grasses and foliage, cutting randomly to avoid bare spots in my perennials or shrubs and quickly placing each stem into a bucket of water.

I began the bouquet with several 12-inch stems of fern pine, or *Podocarpus*, as the stabilizing foliage. Then I added three Shastas, one spray of roses and several about-to-bloom white agapanthus with their pompom-like flowers, including two green pods – quite gorgeous on their thick, erect stems.

Yarrow and an unusual variety of flowering tobacco repeated the yellow daisy centers. It's the extras that add personality, including a few strands of newly unfurled grapevine, several lengths of fragrant jasmine vine and some pinkish plumes of a gorgeous fountain grass.

Simple! To me, successful floral design is about no more than capturing a breathtaking moment in which to observe and marvel at nature's glory. And, of course, there's that other rule: You can never have too many flowers.

Ingredients:
All were harvested from my former garden in Ventura County, California
5 branches fern pine (*Podocarpus gracilior*)
7 stems and pods of lily-of-the-Nile (*Agapanthus* 'Snowy Owl')
1 spray 'Iceberg' rose (*Rosa* 'Iceberg'), a popular floribunda rose
3 vines evergreen jasmine (*Jasminum polyanthum*)
3 stems Shasta daisy (*Leucanthemum* x *superbum*)
5 stems blue tree tobacco (*Nicotiana glauca* 'Salta Blues'), a flowering tobacco with blue-green leaves and long, tubular yellow flowers. This is a cool plant for the perennial border and an equally fetching choice for my bouquet.
7 stems yarrow (*Achillea* 'Moonshine')
9 stems-seed heads fountain grass (*Pennisetum orientale*)
3 grapevines (*Vitis vinifera*)

Vase:
10-inch tall x 7-inch diameter celadon ceramic vase

Seasonal Choices

See the possibilities everywhere: I'm convinced that even the tiniest of gardens can yield interesting and unique flowers, branches, leaves, vines and stems for a seasonal bouquet. You don't have to be a flower farmer to grow and harvest appealing ingredients. And you don't have to be a pro to assemble an eye-pleasing arrangement. Just use your powers of observation to appreciate and experiment with the seasonal beauty around you.

AMERICAN ROSES

PERHAPS IT'S SENTIMENTAL TO ADMIT, but I think the classic bowl of roses is still one of the most beautiful sights to behold in the flower world. Roses are the number one symbol of love when a holiday like Valentine's Day comes around. But there's a huge difference between jumbo South American roses – uniformly bred and grown to withstand long shipping distances – and romantic garden roses that may not last as long in a vase, but are far superior in sensory splendor.

If you are lucky enough to have a rose garden, you know that feeling of excitement when the year's first rosebud appears, then opens, gradually unfurling its soft petals; it's something I cherish until the days when those petals drop to the ground.

I feel a similar thrill when I meet local flower farmers who specialize in garden roses. We yearn for those bodacious flowers, which are more "real" than factory-grown alternatives. I am seduced by their ephemeral quality, by the incredible fragrance and by the way these flowers nod a bit, heads draped over the edge of a vase, rather than standing erect.

Lavender-pink in hue, this 'Wild Blue Yonder' grandiflora rose was grown by Westmont Park Roses, a landscaping and cut flower business in Soap Lake, Washington, about three hours east of Seattle. The owners, John Martin and Robert Salmons, are now harvesting their romantic blooms to supply florists in our area. They gave me these to play with. And play I did, filling a vintage McCoy cachepot with a plum-pink concoction of roses, smoke tree foliage and the dreamy pink form of Queen Anne's lace.

Ingredients:

20 stems *Rosa* 'Wild Blue Yonder' roses, grown by Westmont Park Roses

7 stems smoke tree (*Cotinus coggygria* 'Royal Purple'), grown by Jello Mold Farm

10 stems Queen Anne's lace (*Daucus carota* var. *sativus* 'Black Knight'), grown by J. Foss Garden Flowers

Vase:

7-inch tall x 7½-inch diameter McCoy jardiniere, 1940s era, with a raised design of vertical bands and flowers

From the Farmer

When to cut for the vase: Commercial rose growers like Westmont Park Roses have special procedures for harvesting their flowers and processing them with a hydrating solution before making florist deliveries. The home gardener who grows old English roses and David Austin garden roses isn't faced with these storage and delivery demands. Get the most out of your garden roses by cutting them when temperatures are coolest on the day you plan to arrange them. I like to pick a mix of roses at different stages to create more interest: in bud; slightly open; two-thirds open and fully open. This technique reminds grower John Martin of a single, beautiful grandiflora cluster, "with five or six roses, each at a different blooming cycle."

HEAVENLY HYDRANGEAS

PRISTINE WHITE, PERFECTLY SYMMETRICAL AND VOLUPTUOUS, these hydrangeas are the quintessential summertime flower and a favorite of cottage gardeners and bridal parties.

This is an easy arrangement to create since the mop-head hydrangea blooms cluster together nicely and their relatively straight stems stay upright in a vase. Elegant and long-blooming, they grow on shrubs preferring morning light and afternoon shade. Hydrangeas are surprisingly low-maintenance, even in oppressive heat, if given enough water.

The flowers echo the rounded shape of the celadon-green pottery. The vase's floral pattern reminds me of hydrangea florets, which actually are tiny sterile flowers surrounded by petal-like sepals.

Cut hydrangea stems as long as possible and strip off all leaves. Fill the vase to the rim with water, because hydrangeas soak water through the entire stem, not just from the cut end. Ten mop-head white hydrangeas create this softly mounded design. In search of a lacy accent, I noticed a flash of violet-blue growing just outside my office window: a carefree perennial called *Geranium* 'Rozanne'. Its simple flowers are displayed on long, wiry stems. I tucked a few into the mounded bouquet, allowing 'Rozanne' to cascade over the edge of the vase. Finally, pincushion-like buds of *Scabiosa* add a pleasing texture, echoing the greenish-white of the hydrangeas.

Ingredients:

    10 stems mop-head hydrangeas (*Hydrangea macrophylla*), grown by Oregon Coastal Flowers
    8 stems *Geranium* 'Rozanne', harvested from my garden
    6 stems pincushion flower (*Scabiosa* sp.) in bud, grown by Choice Bulb Farms

Vase:

    11-inch tall x 10-inch diameter ceramic glazed vase (the opening is 5 inches)

From the Farmer

Give your hydrangeas a refreshing drink: Summer-harvested hydrangeas are considered to be shorter-lived than ones cut in autumn, giving them a reputation for not lasting long in a vase. You can revive wilting hydrangea flowers, though. Five days after I made this bouquet, I took the entire arrangement apart, re-cut each hydrangea stem and submerged them in a cool, soaking bath in the kitchen sink for about 15 minutes. With the excess water shaken off, they were refreshed and re-hydrated, guaranteed to last a few more days in the vase.

STUNNING SUCCULENTS

GARDENERS KNOW THAT succulents are versatile and easy-to-grow plants. Both the "leaves" and "flowers" of succulents are now showing up as unexpected elements in vases and bridal bouquets. I was introduced to the nifty technique of treating succulents like cut flowers by several of the talented designers in *The 50 Mile Bouquet*.

When succulents from the garden are paired with flowers from the farm, the results can be quite fetching. The tender varieties like Echeverias, Aeoniums, Graptopetalums, Kalanchoes and Crassulas are among the prettiest to use, although hardy succulents like Sempervivums are also worth trying. The flower-like forms (actually the leaves of the plant) play the role of a "diva" flower, a term I often use to describe dahlias, peonies, roses and other prominent focal blooms. Actual flowers of many succulents are tiny and intricate, dangling from the ends of long, fleshy stems. These, too, can be cut and included in an arrangement.

To transform a living succulent plant into a floral element, cut the rosette from the plant, leaving a stem at least one inch long. Then, insert a short piece of 12-inch gauge floral wire into the cut end. At this stage, some designers prefer to wrap the entire "stem" (the short piece of succulent stem and the floral wire) with adhesive green floral tape, giving it a tidy look. Proceed with your arrangement, including all sorts of rosy, maroon, blue-green, silvery or chartreuse succulents with other seasonal flowers and foliage.

Ingredients for arrangement on opposite page:

Several rosettes from *Echeveria* plants, with wire "stems." I took these cuttings from my friend Cristi Walden's Southern California garden and brought them home to Seattle in my suitcase; they lasted the entire summer in a number of arrangements.

7 stems of rose-red, multi-petal garden roses, variety unknown, harvested from my Seattle garden

Ingredients for arrangement on this page:

Aeonium rosette
Cactus-style summer dahlia

Vase:

6½-inch tall x 4½-inch diameter glass jar with 3½-inch opening

From the Farmer

Succulent success: Robin Stockwell, owner of Succulent Gardens Nursery in Castroville, California, says it's easy to remove rosettes with a clean, sharp florist's knife or clippers. After several days, the succulents will likely be the only part of your bouquet that still looks attractive. They can be re-used in your next arrangement. Or, remove the wire and set the cuttings in a bright window where they'll soon produce roots. That's when you can replant your succulent in a pot or in the garden.

FLIGHTS OF FANCY

I MADE THIS ARRANGEMENT as a hostess gift for my friend Stacie Crooks's annual summer soiree. I know flowers are considered one of the least welcomed hostess gifts (you hand her the bunch and she has to drop everything to find a vase and clippers and assemble it on the spot). But, if you bring a completed arrangement, it's easy for your hostess to set the lovely bouquet on the buffet, kitchen counter or coffee table. I keep a collection of 6-inch round and square glass vases for this reason.

Keep the design low and compact. I began by arranging in my left hand, rotating the bouquet while adding an alternating mix of hot-pink dahlias, goldenrod, lime-green hypericum and lacy-white love-in-a-mist. Once the cluster of flower heads formed a nice dome shape, I inserted several white gooseneck flowers, poking in the stems from the top exactly where I wanted them and reaching beneath the bouquet to pull those stems through. I love fluttery design elements like these that emerge as if they're about to fly away from the other flowers. Finally, I gave the entire a bunch of flowers a green "collar" of interesting foliage – the serrated-edged leaves from a perennial herb called burnet, or *Sanguisorba*.

I re-cut all of the stems to the correct length and placed the bouquet into the vase, fluffing up the flowers a little to settle them in place.

Ingredients:

- 7 stems *Dahlia* 'Coral Gypsy', grown by Jello Mold Farm
- 15 stems white love-in-a-mist *(Nigella damascena)*, grown by J. Foss Garden Flowers
- 5 stems chartreuse *Hypericum perforatum* (a florist's variety selected for its colorful fruit), grown by Jello Mold Farm
- 7 stems goldenrod *(Solidago* sp.), grown by J. Foss Garden Flowers
- 11 stems white gooseneck loosestrife *(Lysimachia clethroides)*, grown by Jello Mold Farm
- 20 stems burnet foliage *(Sanguisorba obtusa)*, grown by Charles Little & Co.

Vase:

6-inch tall x 4-inch diameter glass vase

Eco-technique

Transporting bouquets: Save your arrangement and your car with a smart stabilizing trick I learned from flower farmers who make frequent bouquet deliveries. Use a box that is at least half the height of your vase; seal the top and bottom so you have an empty "cube." Using a utility knife, cut a large X on one side of the box. The cuts should be approximately the same size as the vase diameter. Push the bottom of the vase into the X-opening. The triangular cardboard flaps created by the cuts should bend inward to hold the vase securely while you drive.

PASSION FOR PEONIES

PEONIES IN JULY? Flourishing in the fields of Alaska, no less?

Yes, indeed. At the invitation of several Alaska peony growers, I spent a glorious week at the height of summer visiting fifteen farms between North Pole and Fritz Creek. There is something quite magical that happens in this land of high latitudes, where the summer days last for 22 hours and nighttime is barely acknowledged. The short but intensely bright summers and their ideal conditions of light, temperature, soil and altitude make it possible to grow and harvest peonies at a time when no one else in the world can do so – between the end of June and September.

Once considered old-fashioned, the symbol of Memorial Day, peonies are now an oft-requested

wedding flower. Brides see dreamy bouquets in glossy magazines and they want to carry that romance down the aisle. Until recently, however, peony-themed weddings in late summer were simply not possible.

During the past decade Dr. Patricia Holloway of the University of Alaska at Fairbanks has been conducting peony crop trials at Georgeson Botanic Garden. Her work confirms that peony plants survive Alaska's winters under an insulating blanket of snow only to explode into bloom as soon as things warm up. Her expertise has inspired more than 50 small family farms to plant peonies; increasingly, Alaska is making wedding clients in the lower 48 states very happy – from the DIY bride to the couture floral designer.

I returned from my Alaska tour with visions of peonies dancing in my head, as well as the real deal: boxes of just-picked blooms. Several growers sent me home with their flowers, and frankly, I couldn't bring myself to add a single other botanical element to the vase. What you see here is pure beauty – a perfect bouquet of the season.

Learn more about ordering Alaska-grown peonies at www.alaskapeonies.org.

Ingredients:
    10 stems 'Sorbet' peonies, grown by
        Echo Lake Peonies in Soldotna, Alaska
    5 stems 'Kansas' peonies, grown by
        Midnight Sun Peonies in Soldotna, Alaska

Vase:
    9-inch tall x 7-inch diameter vintage Haegar urn, cream pottery
    or
    Series of vintage one-pint glass milk bottles (7-inch tall), each holding two or three stems

From the Farmer

Peony harvesting and design: Cut peonies during the coolest part of the day. According to Dr. Holloway, "Cut once you see the true color of the flower with one or two petals separating at the top – or any time after that. Then, the flower will continue to open in your arrangement." If you cut prior to this stage the buds either will not open or they will be stunted. Fully-opened blooms can also be harvested, but their vase life is shorter.

Based on years of peony research and field trials, Dr. Holloway offers this commercial growers' tip: "Once cut, your flowers should be chilled in the refrigerator for at least 24 hours and up to one week before putting them into a vase. That chilling very definitely extends vase life." Wrap the peonies in paper towels and lay them flat in the crisper drawer, away from the refrigerator's other contents until use.

UP ON THE ROOF

IF YOUR FLORAL CREATIVITY FEELS LIMITED by a small-scale backyard, take a lesson from my friend Ellen Spector Platt. A gifted author, artist and teacher, Ellen grows a garden in the sky – on the rooftop deck of her New York City condominium. There, ornamental trees, flowering shrubs, a tangle of vines, long-blooming perennials, not to mention tasty herbs and veggies, thrive in containers – an entire botanical garden that Ellen and fellow residents of the highrise enjoy year round.

At Ellen's invitation, I rode the elevator from her building's lobby to the 18th floor garden, where I made this bouquet as she pruned overgrown stems and branches.

So often I'm drawn to flowers, but in this case, the foliage commanded my attention. We snipped the jungle of green-and-pink caladium foliage, arranging five bold leaves to drape over the rim of the pale green vase. Foliage from a bi-colored sage and the golden sumac added more stunning texture. A few stems of glossy green Genovese basil and rosy barberry sprigs repeated the green and dark pink caladium colors. I thought my lush design was complete, until I turned, and there was Ellen, holding a clutch of black-eyed Susan flowers. "What about these?" she suggested. The yellow petals echoed the sumac and even the cream-edged sage. They were the perfect grace note to this summery foliage bouquet.

Ingredients:

All elements were grown by Ellen Spector Platt on the roof of her Manhattan condominium or in the tree pits along the sidewalk by the building's lobby

5 stems *Caladium* x *hortulanum* 'Kathleen'

3 stems bi-color sage (*Salvia officinalis* 'La Crema')

3 stems staghorn sumac (*Rhus typhina* 'Tiger Eyes')

5 stems Genovese basil leaves and flowers (*Ocimum basilicum* 'Genova')

3 stems red-leaf Japanese barberry (*Berberis thunbergii atropurpurea* 'Rose Glow')

7 stems black-eyed Susan (*Rudbeckia fulgida*)

Vase:

8½-inch tall x 7-inch diameter celadon green glass

Eco-technique

Bouquet 2.0: After my visit, Ellen emailed me: "Your arrangement still looks good, but after 4 days it needed some grooming." Here are her tips for reviving a bouquet: "Don't try to groom it by pulling out a wilted stem, since you'll likely take out other good stuff along with it. Instead, leave the stems where they are and reach in to snip off a single dead flower. Or, cut off the entire top of the stem, leaving the bottom in place. No one will ever know it's there." In this arrangement, the black-eyed Susan blooms were the first to be removed.

"By the time many of the stems start to die, I just pick out the few good ones that are left and put them in a narrow vase or bottle to wring out my last bit of enjoyment," says this experienced floral designer. "I'm sure I'll be left with the caladiums, looking like an entirely new design." And sure enough, nine days after we made the original bouquet, Ellen sent me this photo of her green bud vases with the beautiful – and long-lasting – caladium leaves.

SUMMER CONFECTIONS

THE STARS OF THIS ARRANGEMENT are the alluring 'Queen Red Lime' zinnias, an unusual annual that's in such hot demand that many seed companies can't keep the variety in stock. I fell in love with this multicolored zinnia when I produced a floral design story for *Better Homes & Gardens*. It was growing at a flower farm in Cumming, Iowa – and I couldn't resist the arrangement of mauve, lemon-lime and burgundy petals clustered around each stem.

Here in the Pacific Northwest, a few savvy growers procured enough of these seeds for their season, so I was lucky to take home a bunch of 'Queen Red Lime' zinnias for this arrangement. It's uncanny how the zinnia's pale lime petals relate to the buttery- yellow glaze chosen by artist Frances Palmer, who made the vase.

As the pink-and-pale-green palette came together, every botanical element brought the eye back to the zinnias. In bud, the pink dahlia flowers have tight, green centers, which mimic the zinnias in both color and form. Green appears in a variety of appealing textures, including the sprays of sedum, the ninebark's lime-tinged foliage, and the dark green foxtail grass. I assembled the elements in my hand, rotating the bouquet counterclockwise as I worked, tucking the grasses in from the top so they emerged at just the right height. Finally, having placed the bouquet into the vase, I added little sprigs of sedum around the rim – almost like a lacy collar.

Ingredients:

 5 stems *Zinnia elegans* 'Queen Red Lime',
   grown by Jello Mold Farm

 5 stems *Dahlia* 'Rebecca Lynn' in flower and
   bud, grown by Jello Mold Farm

 4 stems *Sedum* 'Green Expectations',
   grown by Jello Mold Farm

 7 blades green millet (*Setaria viridis*), grown
   by Jello Mold Farm

 5 stems golden ninebark (*Physocarpus
   opulifolius* 'Luteus'), grown by Jello Mold
   Farm

Vase:

 8-inch tall x 5-inch diameter fluted vase by
   artist Frances Palmer

Design 101

A very special vase: I was first introduced to the work of Frances Palmer when Stephen Orr profiled the American potter and her Connecticut cutting garden in *Tomorrow's Gardens*. Then Frances appeared on Martha Stewart's television show, where she discussed how she creates her exquisite one-of-a-kind vessels and dinnerware, including vases for the flowers she grows. Her delightful pottery style – classical with a touch of whimsy – is a floral designer's dream come true. Naturally, I set my sights on acquiring one of Frances's pieces. For the vase-lover on a budget, her Pearl Collection reflects the artist's signature style at everyday prices. I chose this fluted vase because of the generous diameter of its opening (nearly 5 inches). And to me, this butter-yellow glaze is a perfect foil for all sorts of flowers, but especially the zinnias and dahlias.

FRUIT AND FLOWERS

BOWLS AND URNS ARE IDEAL for low tabletop arrangements. They evoke the feeling of just-gathered abundance, with tendrils, pods and buds that overflow from the rim. Floral designer Nicole Cordier and I volunteered to donate several arrangements to an event benefitting the non-profit Seattle Children's Play Garden; we employed containers that also were donated for the cause, including a vintage footed Gorham bowl. Offering lots of character and a timeless patina of slightly tarnished silver plate, the vessel called for some old-fashioned flowers, but I also wanted to add a few surprises, like the thorn-free blackberry fruit and the millet seed heads.

We created a loose ball from chicken wire and placed it inside the bowl, securing it with a crisscross of waterproof floral tape. The flowers, foliage, grasses and berries – all donated by Seattle Wholesale Growers Market's vendors – worked nicely with the silver. However, if the bowl had been brass or copper, you can imagine choosing an entirely different group of botanicals.

I began with unevenly placed pieces of the dark-wine ninebark foliage to emerge around the base; the chicken wire openings anchored the short, woody stems in place. Then, a trio of fluffy white hydrangea blossoms – arranged two on one side, one on the other, for an eye-pleasing asymmetry. Next came the beautiful pink 'Abraham Darby' garden roses, placed for a cascade effect and nestled with several 'Queen Red Lime' zinnias. For more draped elements, the millet, unripe berry clusters and a few sprigs of pale lavender-like *Vitex agnus-castus* finished off the voluptuous bowl of blooms.

Ingredients:

- 9 stems ninebark (*Physocarpus opulifolius* 'Diabolo'), grown by Jello Mold Farm
- 3 stems *Hydrangea paniculata* 'Limelight', grown by Oregon Coastal Flowers
- 7 stems 'Abraham Darby', a David Austin English rose grown by Westmont Park Roses
- 7 stems *Zinnia elegans* 'Queen Red Lime', grown by Jello Mold Farm
- 7 blades burgundy millet *(Setaria viridis)*, grown by Charles Little & Co.
- 5 stems thorn-free blackberries *(Rubus fruticosus)*, grown by Charles Little & Co.
- 5 stems *Vitex agnus-castus*, grown by Charles Little & Co.

Vase:

- 7-inch tall x 8-inch diameter vintage Gorham silver plate bowl

Seasonal Choices

Pretty enough to eat: Adding fruit and vegetables to a floral arrangement is a technique as old as the still-life paintings of the 17th century Dutch Masters. The practice has returned and floral designers are harvesting all sorts of edibles from their kitchen gardens and farmers' market stalls. In addition to the yummy blackberries used here, other delicious ingredients can include Alpine strawberries, unripe plums or crab apple fruit on the branch, cherry tomatoes on the vine, colorful Easter egg radishes and bright orange kumquat fruit (insert a wooden pick for easy placement). In general, it's best to use unripe fruit or vegetables, so they last as long as the flowers.

MADE – AND GROWN – IN AMERICA

WHILE SPENDING 52 WEEKS focused on bouquet-making, I also gained an education about the rich history of American pottery. Highly collectible, the vases, urns and vessels that were manufactured between the 1930s and 1960s were originally not that expensive. They were rather humble, utilitarian pieces by makers like McCoy, Haeger, Bauer and Royal Copley – and other ceramics factories that didn't even add an identifying mark on the bottoms of their pieces. Even today, it's relatively affordable to collect the vases that our grandmothers probably had on their shelves; depending on the quality and age, I've spent between $10 and $100 to bring one home.

It's so fitting to pair local and seasonal flowers with American-made pottery. Here are two beautiful vases that I purchased from a dealer in Ohio. The turquoise and green matte finishes, footed details and fluted shapes are perfect complements for two small arrangements.

When you want to showcase a special vase, it's better to simplify its contents. I selected only four ingredients for the two versions: Dahlias, calla lilies, Dusty Miller foliage and Nigella seed pods.

I first inserted the soft, velvety sprigs of Dusty Miller, a garden perennial that is almost evergreen here in the Pacific Northwest. Notice how the silvery leaves look bluer against the turquoise pottery and greener inside the jade-colored vase. Next, I paired dark-fuchsia dahlias with similarly-hued callas, rotating the vase so that the arrangement is balanced on all sides. Their distinct textures look lovely together. Finally, the 'Persian Violet' pods pull it all together, their maroon stripes playing off the flowers – the alternating pale green stripes echoing the foliage.

Ingredients (for each vase):
- 11 stems Dusty Miller *(Centaurea cineraria)*, grown by Charles Little & Co.
- 5 stems *Dahlia* 'Naomi', grown by Jello Mold Farm
- 5 stems 'Hot Lips' calla lilies, grown by Oregon Coastal Flowers
- 12 stems love-in-a-mist *(Nigella damascena* 'Persian Violet')*, grown by Charles Little & Co.

Vases:
- 6¼-inch tall x 5½-inch diameter vintage Haeger vase (green)
- 5¼-inch tall x 5½-inch square vintage McCoy vase (turquoise)

Eco-technique

Green couture: More than ever, floral designers and their customers are adopting green practices, and the vase itself is one important way to be more sustainably-minded. For example, instead of using inexpensive, made-in-China glass floral vases, I opt for something unusual (and usually just as affordable). Great vases can come from flea markets, garage sales, thrift stores and hand-me-downs from relatives. For less than $15 at a time, I purchase a case of one dozen made-in-the-USA Ball canning jars – ideal vases for last-minute gift giving. In fact, I've trained my neighbors to return their jars so I can reuse them for future bouquets.

SEEDPODS AND PETALS

THE DANGLING, CONE-LIKE FLOWERS of common hop suggest autumn's harvest time is just around the corner. Sprays of pearl-sized flax seeds give me the same feeling. The pale blue flower petals of perennial flax *(Linum perenne)* usually drop after one day, which is why it's not a popular cut flower. But look what happens when seeds begin to form! Shimmery-green and textured, the seeded flax is quite attractive. When I used it in a floral demonstration, someone aptly noted: "It's a great improvement over baby's breath!"

At this time of the year, my love affair with zinnias continues; here, I selected a pale green variety to echo the verdant seeds and pods. For contrast, I added ruby-hued masterwort *(Astrantia major)*, a meadow perennial with a pincushion-like flower quite similar to the zinnia's center. This flower will forever remind me of the English gardens I saw when attending the Chelsea Flower Show in England. Masterwort is easy to grow in the cutting border and it dries beautifully. The entire arrangement is gathered into a flower frog resting inside the base of a vintage, creamy-white McCoy urn.

Ingredients:
20 stems perennial flax *(Linum perenne)*, grown by Charles Little & Co.
5 short lengths common hop *(Humulus lupulus)*, grown by Northern Pacific Farm
10 stems lemon-lime zinnias *(Zinnia elegans* 'Queen Lime'), grown by Everyday Flowers
12 stems masterwort *(Astrantia major)*, grown by Ojeda Farms

Vases:
4½-inch tall x 4½-inch wide x 8-inch long rectangular vintage McCoy vase

Grow This

Instant gratification: I had been waiting all summer to use hop vines and their dangling green cones in an arrangement. These stems came from Oregon. Floral designers love the dreamy, 18-foot-long hop garlands, often using them to decorate wedding arbors. Common hop is also used by home brewers. With fast-growing, twining stems, hand-sized lobed leaves and bract-like flowers, the female form of *Humulus lupulus* is also a "quick" screen for a fence, wall or trellis. It does, however, need to be cut back once a year (usually in late fall, after the first frost), in order to produce a new flush of vines the following season.

AUTUMN

*It would be worthwhile having a cultivated garden
if only to see what Autumn does to it.*

– Alfred Austin

One moment the borders and flower beds are overly abundant, filled with vibrant hues and untamed, billowy perennials. Almost overnight, the days begin to shorten; nighttime lengthens. Our eyes adjust to the fading palette of spent blooms and leaves. The barren and beautiful architecture of trees and shrubs is soon revealed. There's an intricacy to fall's foliage, pods, seeds and branches – all of which take on a heightened importance in the vase. I'm reminded that it's not all about blooms and I embrace the crumbling loveliness of it all. The cycle of nature has come full circle.

Gifts from the wild fields and the urban fringes are readily available. I gather leaves and tie them in bunches to festoon my front porch. I fill a woven basket with pinecones, acorns or chestnuts, dropped from trees in my neighborhood. After a windstorm, I collect downed twigs and bundle them to stand upright in an urn on the fireplace threshold.

The autumn bouquet created with a "slow flowers" approach is unapologetically seasonal. Petals have fallen from my favorite perennial, leaving only naked seed heads. Moss and lichen soften the rough edges of ancient-looking bark. Elderly leaves take on a burnished patina that artists have tried for years to perfect on their canvases.

When observed in a new way, autumn's spare details are a wonderful source of creativity.

AUTUMN'S FADING HUES

THE INGREDIENTS IN THIS LUSH, OVERFLOWING ARRANGEMENT hint that summer is vanishing. Here is fall! The burnished urn, the tawny flowers and foliage – even the just-harvested vine tomatoes clipped from the kitchen garden – suggest a moment hovering somewhere between the seasons.

This bouquet is definitely local and seasonal, but true confession: I procured one-half of the ingredients in Seattle on the morning that I hopped an airplane for San Francisco to teach a "Slow Flowers" workshop. Picture me passing through airport security as TSA officers admired my armload of flowers.

The remaining floral elements came from Bay Area farms and gardens, including some grown by Baylor Chapman, owner of Lila B. Design, a popular eco-floral design studio. Baylor contributed pittosporum, coneflower seed heads and other goodies from her parking-lot cutting garden. And my workshop host, Lizzy Jackson of the Hillsborough Garden Club, clipped and shared branches of dark plum foliage from her smoke bush.

As with most shallow containers, I installed a loosely-formed mound of chicken wire and secured it in place with dark green floral tape. Then I added the garden foliage, alternating short stems of the plum-colored smoke bush with the light green pittosporum so their tips draped over the urn's rim. Next, I added the medium-sized ingredients: apricot-colored dahlias, terracotta-orange lily stems and pale peach stock. These elements contribute to the bouquet's lushness, but its visual interest really took shape with the inclusion of wild-looking seed heads: millet, perennial flax, rose hips, spent euphorbia blooms and coneflowers. Those fine and rough textures hover above the flowers and foliage, inviting the viewer to peer closer to discover what's beneath them. As a final touch, as I was walking through hostess Marritje Green's garden, I noticed some beautiful yellow pear tomatoes on the vine. I tucked a stem into the front of the bouquet, between two dahlias – a perfect grace note, reminding me that harvest time is here.

Ingredients:
   7 stems smoke tree (*Cotinus coggygria* 'Grace'), harvested from Lizzy
      Jackson's garden
   7 stems pittosporum (*Pittosporum* sp.), harvested from the Lila B. lot
      garden
   5 stems *Dahlia* 'Hy Suntan', grown by Jello Mold Farm
   5 stems gold and pale pink garden roses, harvested from the Lila B.
      lot garden
   3 stems terracotta-orange lilies (*Lilium* 'Olina Tango'™), grown by
      Peterkort Roses
   5 stems pale peach stock (*Matthiola incana*), grown by Repetto's Nursery
   7 stems perennial flax (*Linum perenne*), grown by Charles Little
      & Co.
   7 stems brown millet (*Setaria viridis* 'Caramel'), grown by Charles Little & Co.
   Miscellaneous seed heads, harvested from the Lila B. lot garden, including purple coneflower
      (*Echinacea purpurea*), *Euphorbia* sp., and rose hips
   2 clusters yellow pear tomatoes, harvested from Marritje Green's garden

Vase:
   7-inch tall x 10-inch diameter antique-finish urn with 6½-inch opening

Eco-technique

A fresh drink of water: There's a proliferation of advice for keeping a bouquet of floral ingredients fresh and lasting for many days. But one of the most important things you can do is give stems clean water. That's not so easy with an arrangement like this one, where all the stems are knit together in a tangle of chicken wire. My friend Lorene Edwards Forkner shared this easy water-changing trick: Place the entire arrangement in the kitchen sink. Gently lift the foliage at one edge of the vase so the faucet's spray nozzle is directed inside. Turn on the water and let it flow for a minute or two. The existing water will begin to overflow and go down the drain, displaced by fresh water that now occupies the vase (dry off the bottom and outside of the container when finished). Do this every day or two for the life of the arrangement.

RHYTHM IN GLASS

ARTIST TRACY GLOVER'S one-of-a-kind lighting pieces and decorative vases are adorned with all sorts of intriguing motifs. When she asked if I wanted to create a bouquet to pair with one of her vessels, I couldn't resist her Licorice Stick vase with ribbon-like bands of glass in gorgeous hues. I love Tracy's color sensibility and was inspired by this vase's chocolate brown, wheat gold, lime green, pale teal and dark blue palette. The streaks form a beautiful, graphic pattern that wraps around the cylindrical vase.

I wanted to arrange a mostly upright bouquet so the botanical ingredients wouldn't obscure the fine glasswork. Chocolate cosmos came immediately to mind as a seasonal flower to emphasize but not overpower the vase's rich brown detailing. This charming annual, with 1½-inch mocha-merlot petals arranged around sooty centers, is highly valued by gardeners and floral designers alike. I was lucky to source a generous bunch of chocolate cosmos from Katherine Anderson, a doubly-gifted farmer-florist who owns Seattle's Marigold and Mint.

Pale apricot snapdragons contrast with the dark cosmos, while pink-plumed celosia repeats the wheat-gold banding. Finely textured geranium leaves echo the vase's lime streaks.

Like hearing two voices that harmonize beautifully, there's a pleasing sensory experience when the vertical lines of the flower stems and the vase's horizontal bands come together. It's a winning combination of flowers and glass.

Ingredients:

7 stems fancy-leaf scented geranium (*Pelargonium crispum*), grown by Charles Little & Co.

3 stems pale apricot snapdragons (*Antirrhinum majus*), grown by Everyday Flowers

7 stems (tips only) light peach cockscomb (*Celosia plumosa*), grown by Charles Little & Co.

15 stems chocolate cosmos (*Cosmos atrosanguineus*), grown by Marigold and Mint

Vase:

8-inch tall x 4-inch diameter hand-blown art glass vase, designed by Tracy Glover

Design 101

Dark and light: When you place lighter or brighter flowers around darker floral elements, the viewer's attention is drawn to the distinct details of both. Here, the chocolate cosmos looks even better because it is displayed next to lighter-hued companion flowers: pale apricot snapdragons.

TO GRACE MY KITCHEN COUNTER

THE HAND-THROWN, BISQUE-COLORED POTTERY was a wedding gift from a law colleague of my husband's. I've always loved this piece, but for nearly 30 years the bowl has been displayed in a dining room hutch – admired, but not considered functional for serving food.

Then I brought home these gorgeous pink and coral elements from the Growers Market and the quiet bowl grabbed my attention. I realized it was ideal for a low floral arrangement. It has a certain polish, thanks to the detailed "foot" and beautiful glaze.

I used a round metal flower frog inside the bowl and began by adding three fine-textured green elements. Each one has loads of interest: the button-shaped Boltonia seed heads, the heathery Artemisia and the lacy scented geranium leaves.

Into the soft base of green I placed coral-pink crested cockscomb and a playful form of apricot zinnias. I placed the almost-forgotten pottery on my kitchen counter – a perfect companion to the botanically-inspired tiles made by my friend Paula Gill of Red Step Studio.

Ingredients:
    5 stems fancy-leaf scented geranium (*Pelargonium crispum*), grown by Charles Little & Co.
    7 stems *Boltonia asteroides*, a small daisy-like perennial, grown by Charles Little & Co.
    7 stems *Artemisia capillaris*, a woody perennial, grown by Charles Little & Co.
    6 stems pink crested cockscomb (*Celosia cristata*), grown by Charles Little & Co.
    9 stems apricot cactus zinnias (*Zinnia elegans* 'Pinca'), grown by J. Foss Garden Flowers

Vase:
    4½-inch tall x 6¼-inch diameter hand-thrown clay bowl

Design 101

The power of green: The difference between one arrangement being just pretty and another being completely arresting is often not the flowers but the foliage. You see here that three similar-toned green elements are woven together as a textured and verdant tapestry. They are definitely the supporting actors to the zinnia and cockscomb divas, but they help this bouquet sing. Whenever you can use unexpected greenery, your design will take on a similar star quality. Often, these elements come straight from the garden – growing right under our noses.

OLD WORLD MEETS NEW FLOWERS

LARGE ENOUGH TO BE USED as a terrarium, my green glass jar is one of two I purchased from a local antique shop at the urging of designer friend Jean Zauptil. The size and shape, not to mention the irregular shape of the rim, were immediately appealing, especially when we learned these were vintage oil jars from Portugal.

Because of its scale, this vessel required taller floral elements that wouldn't look lost inside it. I filled the jar's 5½-inch opening with nine long stems of *Sedum* 'Autumn Joy'. Their huge flower heads are dense and dome-shaped, allowing the sedum mound to act as a botanical flower frog through which other ingredients can be added. This was especially helpful since the bells of Ireland stems weren't long enough to touch the bottom of the container and they needed to appear taller than they really were.

Supported by the sedum flower heads, the apple green spires look great and are still able to get a drink of water from below. Chocolate sunflowers dance lightly among the bells of Ireland, providing a nice complement to the sedums' rust-pink hue. Three fruiting crab apple branches remind us that it is autumn: a harvest welcome to those arriving on our front porch.

Ingredients:
9 stems *Sedum* 'Autumn Joy', grown by J. Foss Garden Flowers
7 stems bells of Ireland (*Moluccella laevis*), grown by J. Foss Garden Flowers
7 stems chocolate sunflowers (*Helianthus annuus* 'Moulin Rouge'), grown by J. Foss Garden Flowers
3 branches fruiting crab apple (*Malus* 'Professor Sprenger'), harvested by Jello Mold Farm

Vase:
13-inch tall x 9-inch diameter with 5½-inch opening, vintage Portuguese oil jar

Eco-technique

Botanical elements as flower frogs: I often start an arrangement using soft, fluffy foliage or dense flowers like the *Sedum* 'Autumn Joy' as the "base" that peeks out over the top of the rim. Once the stabilizing element is in place, all the other stems can be inserted through it and they will remain just where you want them. The foliage and flowers are integral to the overall composition and there's no need for florist's foam.

CLUSTERS OF PINK

I'VE PAIRED YET ANOTHER vintage container with this week's bouquet. It was gifted to me by Jean Zaputil, whom I've called my "garden muse" since she taught me how to garden in the 1980s. Jean arrived one day, saying: "I thought you'd like this Floraline vase – it's what flower shops used before they switched to clear glass."

The olive-green pedestal vase has an elongated opening that is ideal for an arrangement that will be viewed from one side because it accommodates lots of outward-facing stems. But I think it also would be pretty with a symmetrical arrangement of flowers, to be admired on both sides.

I started by clipping several small hydrangea heads from my garden. At this time of year – early October – Seattle hasn't had its first frost. Plants in my garden are transitioning to dormancy, which for hydrangeas means taking on a beautiful, antiqued patina. Two months earlier, the flower heads were vivid baby blue. Now, they have touches of lavender, powder blue and silver in their petals. Still lovely, perhaps in a quieter way.

The hydrangeas go in first, their stems clipped short so the flower heads rest low in the vase. Next, I inserted several branches from one of my favorite autumn-interest plants: snowberry. You often see this native shrub that produces pearly-white berries, but Oregon flower farmers Charles and Bethany Little grow a variety that produces lavender-pink ones. Clustered informally in groups of two or three, the berry-laden stems emerge above the hydrangeas on both sides of the bouquet.

Then, perhaps some of the season's final dahlias. I never tire of using these generous "team players" in my vases. Long-lasting, with dramatic forms and a wide-ranging palette, dahlias elevate every other flower in the vase. When I bought this bunch from grower Vivian Larson, of Everyday Flowers, she mentioned worrying that frost was just around the corner. Smart flower farmers like Vivian extend the dahlia season by a week or two by planting some varieties in protective high tunnels or harvesting dahlias just before temperatures drop – and storing them in coolers for up to a week.

I used Vivian's flamingo-pink dahlias as a central design element, clustering five of them in a quincunx arrangement. Tiny globe amaranths finish off the bouquet. They're tucked in clusters here and there between the other blooms, adding texture like embroidered French knots on the bodice of a dress.

Ingredients:
4 stems hydrangea (*Hydrangea macrophylla*), harvested from my garden
9 stems pink snowberry (*Symphoricarpos* x *doorenbosii* 'Amethyst'), grown by Charles Little & Co.
5 stems *Dahlia* 'Nijinsky', grown by Everyday Flowers
15 stems globe amaranth (*Gomphrena globosa*), grown by Charles Little & Co.

Vase:
6-inch tall x 7-inch wide x 4-inch deep vintage Floraline florist's vase

Design 101

Group for impact: Tiny flowers can disappear when they are added to a bouquet with mostly larger blooms. One of the ways to give them more impact is to group three or five into a mini-bouquet, tied with bind wire or string. When added to the bouquet, the small cluster reads as a color block that's more noticeable in the overall composition. Here, I wired together several sets of the clover-like globe amaranth flowers and inserted them between the much-larger hydrangea and dahlia blooms.

HAPPY HALLOWEEN

IF ANY DATE ON THE CALENDAR is associated with a single color, it has to be the pairing of October 31st with pumpkin orange.

With that in mind, I remembered two vintage McCoy vessels that Jean Zaputil and I purchased at a rummage sale. She snagged the flower pot with its raised pattern and built-in saucer; I brought home the slender, fluted bud vase. It's impressive that the 50-year-old containers' burnt orange glaze is still in pristine condition. Someone else cherished these for a long time before they came into our hands.

Orange shows up in a lot of flower fields this time of year, when planted rows explode with everything from plump, multi-petal marigolds to delicate, butterfly-like crocosmias. I like the interplay of using two distinctly different flower shapes with an identical color.

An ornamental fountain grass lends a festive touch. This one is reminiscent of Independence Day sparklers, and its inflorescences definitely add shimmer. Greenery breaks up the intense orange of both the vases and the flowers. I used wonderful-smelling stems of fresh mint (thoughts of those summertime mojitos tease me when I get a whiff).

Finally, the dots of buttercream-yellow feverfew, a chrysanthemum relative, repeat the marigolds' rounded flower heads. Feverfew is one of my favorite accent flowers, compatible with both cool and warm-toned compositions.

Ingredients:

I used a combination of these floral ingredients in the two bouquets:

Culinary mint (*Mentha* sp.), grown by J. Foss Garden Flowers

Marigolds (*Tagetes erecta*), grown by J. Foss Garden Flowers

Crocosmia x *crocosmiiflora* 'Emily McKenzie', grown by J. Foss Garden Flowers

Fountain grass (*Miscanthus sinensis* 'Rotsilber'), grown by Jello Mold Farm

Feverfew (*Tanacetum parthenium* 'Vegmo Lime'), grown by Everyday Flowers

Vase:

6-inch tall x 4-inch diameter vintage McCoy bud vase

Flower pot:

5¼-inch tall x 5-inch diameter vintage McCoy flower pot

Grow This

Ornamental grasses: Autumn is the best time of year to harvest ornamental grasses and grains for inclusion in bouquets. Right after the fountain grass, foxtail grass and millet bloom, when the heads are still ripe, cut the slender grass stems and place in fresh water until used in an arrangement. If you harvest grasses after the seed heads have begun to dry, they tend to shatter, leaving little seeds all over your tablecloth.

MARKET FRESH

SOMETIMES, LESS IS MORE. That's certainly the case here. This tall bouquet, ideal for an entry table or doorway, looks a lot like those buckets of flowers sold at the farmers' market. I collect old and new French flower buckets because they are quite useful for organizing stems from my cutting garden – and perfect as impromptu vases.

This lovely mix of gold, orange and red dahlias was given to me by dahlia farmer Dan Pearson. Owner of Dan's Dahlias, the 38-year-old husband and father of two has raised and sold dahlias since he was ten years old. That's when customers who drove past the family dairy farm in Oakville, Washington, regularly stopped to buy Dan's one-dollar bunches of dazzling red, pink, orange and purple dahlias. Today, you can find Dan and his dahlias at the Olympia Farmers' Market, Washington's second-largest public market. Or, like thousands of gardeners and dahlia enthusiasts around the country, you can order dahlia tubers direct from his web site.

Other locally-grown autumn elements play nicely with the dahlias, include the blooming fountain grass, egg-yolk yellow crocosmia and a few heads of ornamental millet. The elements in this bouquet come together to create a bright spot – all the more appreciated because they help to put a face on the men and women who grew them.

Ingredients:

20 stems *Dahlia* 'Audrey Grace',
'Keith H' and 'Pearson's Patrick',
grown by Dan's Dahlias

5 stems fountain grass
(*Miscanthus sinensis*), grown by
Jello Mold Farm

5 stems yellow crocosmia
(*Crocosmia* sp.), grown by
J. Foss Garden Flowers

6 stems millet (*Setaria italica* 'Red
Jewel'), grown by Charles Little
& Co.

Vase:

13-inch tall x 7-inch diameter
galvanized metal flower bucket

Grow This

Dazzled by dahlias: Perhaps it's because of their amazing diversity in color, form, petal shape and size, but the dahlia is no longer just an old-fashioned cottage flower. It's an in-demand ingredient for brides, hosts and floral designers who can't seem to get enough of this plant that originated in the highland areas of Mexico and Central America. "They vary in size from less than two inches to ten inches," Dan Pearson points out. "People are drawn to those dinner-plate-sized flowers for the wow factor, but soon they realize that the smaller to medium-sized flowers are useful for bouquets." You can learn a lot more about growing and harvesting dahlias at www.dansdahlias.com.

TARNISHED AND TEXTURED

WITH THE GROWING POPULARITY of terrariums, gardeners, crafters and floral designers have discovered a quirky relative of the bromeliad. It's called *Tillandsia*, or air plant.

These plants are epiphytes, which means most do not grow in soil but draw nutrients and moisture from fog, dew and precipitation. Sculptural and oddly beautiful, a single tillandsia looks stunning on its own, displayed in a shallow dish of pebbles. In more temperate places like Southern California or

Hawaii, tillandsias can be left outdoors, tucked into the crook of a tree branch or hung like ornaments on a chain. Where it's colder, they need to come inside for the winter. My favorite tillandsia, seen here in a silver-and-green composition, typically hangs in the bathroom where it appreciates the humidity of a steaming shower.

This arrangement is unique because it doesn't require water. It's an assemblage of tactile and uncommon "found objects" from nature that will look beautiful for months, displayed on a coffee table or counter. The tillandsia's ghostly leaves arch outward from the base of the plant, draping nicely over the rim of a chipped cast-iron planter. I continued the textural design theme with several tiny green-speckled Tennessee dancing gourds and greenish-white Japanese nest egg gourds, grown locally in fields alongside Cinderella pumpkins and ornamental squashes. I love their twisted stems and interesting shapes.

Finally, I inserted a favorite punctuation point: ping-pong-shaped *Scabiosa stellata* pods, which last forever when dried. Their papery bronze texture is well suited for the paint-chipped urn and its contents.

Ingredients:
- 1 *Tillandsia xerographica* plant, a gift from Nan Sterman (Tillandsias benefit from a light spritzing of water every week or so)
- 3 Japanese nest egg gourds, grown by Jello Mold Farm
- 5 Tennessee dancing gourds, grown by Jello Mold Farm
- 9 stems *Scabiosa stellata* 'Paper Moon', grown by J. Foss Garden Flowers

Vase:
- 5½-inch tall x 16-inch long x 6-inch wide, vintage cast-iron planter, found at the Long Beach Flea Market

Design 101

Balance, a design principle: Balance is deeply ingrained in our psyches. In the garden or in a vase, a visually-balanced design feels pleasing to the eye; when something feels out of balance, it can be agitating to look at. Balance is divided into three categories: Asymmetrical (seen here), in which both halves of a composition may express similar visual weight but are unevenly positioned. Balance is created by a shift in weight on either side of a central fulcrum. Here, you see that the left side of the arrangement reveals the decorative handle of my urn, while the right side of the arrangement offsets it with the curved leaves of the tillandsia. Symmetrical or bilateral balance means that both sides of a composition are equal, one side essentially mirroring the opposite side. Formal flower arrangements are often symmetrical. Radial balance emanates from a central core, like the rays of a sunflower or spokes of a wheel. This dynamic approach appears in perfectly-domed bridal bouquets or centerpieces designed for 360-degree viewing.

VINTAGE PATINA

MY AUTUMN DECOR SCHEME relies on the many hydrangeas that I cut and bring indoors. I love how they turn dusky amethyst or verdigris blue-green as the season winds down. At this point, their stems last much longer in a vase than in the middle of summer.

To make this arrangement, I selected a favorite cast-iron urn, slightly aged and a little rusty. Since it has a drainage hole and is intended for outdoor plants, I lined it with a plastic bowl to create a watertight vessel. Inside, a rounded piece of chicken wire holds short stems in place.

About one dozen hydrangeas fill the opening and form a soft floral mound. This full look called for a "collar" of foliage as a finishing touch. I chose silvery-gray Dusty Miller leaves *(Centaurea cineraria)*, which draped nicely over the urn's edge (the 4-inch leaf stems are just long enough to insert in the hidden chicken wire). Taller stems of sea oats *(Chasmanthium latifolium)*, an ornamental grass, give the design its height. It's easy to poke them through the hydrangeas and watch the flat seed heads dance above, almost as if an autumn breeze is blowing through a meadow.

Ingredients:

- 12 stems mop-head hydrangeas (*Hydrangea macrophylla*), harvested from my garden (note, the lace-cap hydrangeas don't have the same visual impact as the mop-head form)
- 20 stems Dusty Miller (*Centaurea cineraria*), grown by Charles Little & Co.
- 25 stems sea oats (*Chasmanthium latifolium*), grown by Jello Mold Farm

Vase:

- 7-inch tall x 11-inch diameter cast-iron urn. Intended as a planter, it converts to a watertight vase when lined with a plastic bowl.

Eco-technique

Preserve your bouquet: There's a bonus to using these late-season flowers in an arrangement. As the vase water slowly evaporates, the mop-head hydrangeas, Dusty Miller foliage and sea oats will air-dry without changing shape or color. I created the arrangement you see here during the first week of November and by the following May it looked just about the same. By then, I needed the urn for another project, so I disassembled the preserved ingredients and tossed them in the compost bin. Not every cut flower will air-dry as nicely as this trio did, but with a little experimentation you'll soon notice that some long-lasting ingredients can be preserved for months.

A (LOVING) CUP FULL OF AUTUMN

THE LAST FLOWERS OF SUMMER are often reluctant to disappear come fall, which is why I was fortunate to procure Jello Mold Farm's final crop of 'Cafe au Lait' dahlias for this vivid bouquet. Several full-figure 'Piano Freiland' roses, grown in Oregon greenhouses, add polish to this otherwise rustic arrangement. Glistening red rose hips, branches of burnished leaves and green millet are reminders of the fruits of the harvest.

This is a time of year when the sun lowers in the sky and things takes on a metallic hue. Perhaps that's why I selected my tarnished silver loving cup as a vase. This is no ordinary tennis or swimming trophy. Look close to read its inscription: "Woman's Club of Hollywood Flower Show 1917." My writer-friend Kathryn Renner spotted this piece in an online auction. She sent me a note saying: "If you don't bid on it, I will." So I did!

With these lovely dahlias, the arrangement practically designed itself, as my friend Julie Chai would say. Start with an odd number of dahlias and roses, arranging them in a compact grouping to rest just above the opening of the trophy cup. Then, add woody elements so they emerge above and to the sides of the softer blooms. Green millet is ideal because it naturally spills over the rim of a vase. The draping seed heads balance the upright oak and rose hip branches – an armload of autumn!

Ingredients:
- 5 stems *Rosa* 'Piano Freiland', grown by Peterkort Roses
- 3 stems *Dahlia* 'Cafe au Lait', grown by Jello Mold Farm
- 9 blades green millet (*Setaria italica* 'Highlander'), grown by Jello Mold Farm
- 3 stems scarlet oak foliage (*Quercus coccinea*), grown by Oregon Coastal Flowers
- 3 stems wild rose hips, harvested by Oregon Coastal Flowers

Vase:
- 10½ inch tall x 4-inch diameter vintage silver loving cup (look for old trophies at thrift stores or online auctions; or perhaps you'll find one in the family that has personal meaning).

Design 101

A floral designer's recipe: To create a classic floral arrangement, I need ingredients to fulfill three purposes. First, I choose the diva – an eye-catching, dramatic bloom with a symmetrical or dome-shaped form, such as a rose, peony or dahlia. Then I add taller ingredients to emerge from the main cluster of diva flowers. Flowering, fruiting or foliage-laden branches are ideal – I consider them the arrangement's exclamation point. Finally, I add softer elements to drape over the edge of the vase, dripping like chandelier crystals.

LEAVES, BRANCHES, BERRIES AND BLOOMS

THIS ARRANGEMENT INCLUDES ELEMENTS that I gleaned from my garden, combined with botanicals from local growers. It is the ideal dinner party centerpiece because it is long, low and interesting from both sides.

I started with a rustic container: a tarnished aluminum planter that I found at a tag sale. It has a scalloped outline that made me think it could hold 3 pots of herbs. Since it was watertight, I didn't have to create a liner. Loosely-formed chicken wire fills all three sections, into which I placed stems and branches.

Smooth, blue-green eucalyptus created the first layer. I arranged pieces to drape over the container's edge where the silvery-green foliage blends nicely with the weathered metal.

Then I added a mix of low and tall ingredients. I used oak-leaf hydrangea leaves for their gorgeous form and fall color, purple beautyberry and red rose hips. Seed heads appear from the centers of purple coneflowers and papery-crisp *Scabiosa stellata*. I've also added a touch of elegance with pale lime 'Supergreen' roses, their stems cut short so they integrate with the foliage and berries.

Ingredients:

- 20 stems smooth eucalyptus foliage (*Eucalyptus gunnii*), grown by Charles Little & Co.
- 5 large leaves from oak leaf hydrangea *(Hydrangea quercifolia)*, harvested from my garden
- 10 stems purple beautyberry (*Callicarpa bodinieri* var. *giraldii* 'Profusion'), grown by Charles Little & Co.
- 7 stems rose hips (*Rosa multiflora*), grown by Charles Little & Co.
- 7 purple coneflower seed heads (*Echinacea purpurea*), harvested from my garden
- 5 stems pincushion flower seed heads (*Scabiosa stellata* 'Paper Moon'), grown by J. Foss Garden Flowers
- 7 stems 'Supergreen' hybrid tea roses (*Rosa* 'Supergreen'), grown by Peterkort Roses

Vase:

- 5-inch tall x 17-inch long aluminum planter with three 6-inch wide planting sections

Grow This

Garden for foliage: Perennials and shrubs produce some of the most interesting "greenery" for DIY floral designers. Clipping leafy branches from your own backyard is obviously more economical than buying foliage. But it also means the difference between a prosaic bouquet and one with loads of personality. Unique silver, burgundy, gold and blue-green leaves of all sizes and textures lend garden-inspired style to your designs.

I'LL TAKE FLOWERS IN ANY FORM

ANYONE WHO ENTERS A GARDEN CENTER in late autumn is faced with a limited selection of options for their container plants. Ubiquitous winter pansies, autumn asters and colorful mums fill the racks. Then there are pots of ornamental cabbage and kale. We rely on these plants to jazz up containers on our patios and front porches at a time when there's less going on in our gardens.

And now, you may begin seeing kale in floral arrangements. Flower farmers are growing this winter-hardy member of the *Brassica* clan, choosing varieties with extra-long stems and pretty, ruffled leaves. Once the outer petals are removed, the plant's dense center resembles a giant cabbage rose, albeit 4 inches in diameter.

As a challenge to myself, I brought a bunch home from the Growers Market. Wondering what to pair with them, my eyes landed on the tricolor sage from the same grower, Charles Little of Oregon's Willamette Valley. A dusting of plum emerges on the margins of the herb's variegated green-and-white leaves and stems – a perfect accent for the kale "blooms." I arranged the elements in a low green planter, making sure I lined it with a plastic bowl, to hold water, and a flower frog. Several rose-like kale heads are situated low and compact to emerge just above the container's opening. The sage sprigs fill spaces around the rim of the container and between the larger "flowers"; together, the colors and textures combine to turn these ordinary elements into a surprisingly attractive bouquet.

Ingredients:
  7 stems pink flowering kale (*Brassica oleracea*),
    trimmed to resemble a bloom, grown by
    Charles Little & Co.
  20 stems tricolored sage (*Salvia officinalis*
    'Tricolor'), grown by Charles Little & Co.

Vase:
  5-inch tall x 10-inch diameter with 6-inch
    opening vintage ceramic planter

Grow This

Herbs for foliage: Herbs of all kinds – herbaceous or woody – make excellent greenery in floral arrangements. When you think about it, this comes as no surprise. Culinary herbs last for days when we clip them from the kitchen garden and bring inside, plunking a few stems into a jar of water until we're ready to start cooking. My "aha" herb moment occurred while on a photo shoot at a U-Pick farm. The photographer was waiting and I quickly needed to find dark foliage as contrast for a vase of zinnias. Fortunately for me, the farm's herb patch was filled with dark purple basil plants and they looked (and smelled) wonderful in that bouquet.

CONIFERS, CONES AND HOTHOUSE LILIES

AUTUMN WALKS FILL MY POCKETS with interesting cones, chestnuts and pods, gifts from nature that I gather from the ground. I love to display them in baskets and bowls as a reminder of the season. And sometimes nature gives me entire branches – like spruce boughs with dangling cones that a windstorm knocked down. Dropped from a neighbor's tall tree into my driveway, they inspired this conifer bouquet that graced our dining room's side table for the holidays.

The turquoise glaze of a grand urn coaxes hints of blue-green from the spruce and several sprays of Western red cedar that I added to arrangement. I incorporated some glossy elements, too: a few branches from a camellia shrub in our yard and lengths of variegated ivy that hangs over a neighboring fence.

Nicole Cordier, manager at the Seattle Wholesale Growers Market, handed me this lovely raspberry-and-white bunch of long-stemmed lilies as a holiday gift. Each stem bore at least five plump flower buds ready to explode as soon as I added them to the vase of conifers. This floral palette of dark pink and teal is a modern twist on Christmas red-and-green, just as festive and definitely a reminder of the gifts of nature.

Ingredients:

- 5 stems dark pink 'Rio Negro' hybrid Oriental lilies, greenhouse grown by Peterkort Roses
- 5 stems Norway spruce *(Picea abies)*, gleaned from my driveway
- 7 short branches Western red cedar *(Thuja plicata)*, clipped from my garden
- 3 stems Camellia *(Camellia japonica)*, clipped from my garden
- 5 lengths variegated ivy *(Hedera helix)*, trimmed from a neighbor's fence

Vase:

- 12-inch tall x 9-inch diameter with 6-inch opening vintage McCoy urn

Design 101

Lilies for longevity: When you design with Oriental lilies, more than a week of enjoyment will ensue. One or two blooms at a time open and share their loveliness almost in succession, ensuring that something is always in flower. Don't forget to clip the pollen-laden stamen and pistils from the center of each bloom as it opens. Otherwise, as those pieces fall, they can stain table linens.

WINTER

One must maintain a little bit of summer,
even in the middle of winter.

–Henry David Thoreau

Breathtaking beauty is discovered in winter's silent moments – when frost, chill or snow arrives. We live in a suspended state of anticipation – beginning with the winter solstice and continuing until spring's equinox. In between, there are thirteen weeks during which our gardens and much of nature sleeps, gathering important resources for the growth spurt to come. To live intentionally "in season" causes many floral designers to stretch their creativity. It is a quieter palette with which we work, less obvious than during the rest of the year.

I am grateful for this experience, one that has introduced me to the inherent splendor of leafless branches. The brilliant color we expect from the garden during the warmer months recedes, presenting a rich, textured, evergreen landscape. Blooms, when they come, are modest rather than outrageous. The gifts of winter are all the more valuable because of their rareness.

The calendar welcomes a New Year. The dormant earth yields unexpected surprises that range from flame-colored dogwood branches to red-pink winter camellias…no less elegant than the summer perennial border, but distinguished by the pure, poignant landscape of this hushed season.

Bare branches are highly useful in winter season floral decor. And when the buds on those twigs begin to swell, there's a little promise that springtime is on the horizon. This simply gorgeous wreath of magnolia branches was made by Oregon Coastal Flowers, a sustainable farm specializing in callas, hydrangeas and woodland crops.

ILEX BERRIES AND PAPER WHITES

WELCOME TO THE HOLIDAY SEASON, when flowers are less likely to originate from my outdoor garden and more likely to be forced indoors. The lovely tradition of potting up paper whites *(Narcissus papyraceus)*, a spring-flowering daffodil cherished for its intensely fragrant flowers, can't come at a better time for most of us. Far removed from the outdoor landscape, it only takes a handful of bulbs nestled up to their necks in potting soil (plus a sunny windowsill) to "force" their green blades and stems into premature flower production.

I created this red-and-green display as a modern alternative to the expected poinsettia centerpiece. Five paper white bulbs, planted in a shallow dish, occupy the center of a metal-lined (waterproof) wicker tray. I surrounded the dish with a wreath of chicken wire into which I inserted the "greenery," aka velvety geranium foliage. The leaves obscured the wire framework and circled the bulbs as they continued to grow and flower. Finally, I poked berry-laden branches of Oregon-grown *Ilex* to stand upright in the leafy geranium base. By occasionally adding fresh water to the greenery and bulbs, I enjoyed this arrangement for several weeks.

Ingredients:

5 paper white bulbs (*Narcissus papyraceus*), available at many garden centers beginning in autumn. I like to plant pots of these bulbs indoors around Thanksgiving so that their blooms (and scent) fill the house by the December holidays.

20 stems scented geranium foliage (*Pelargonium citrosum*), grown by Charles Little & Co.

10 stems winter berry (*Ilex verticillata*), grown by Charles Little & Co.

Vase:

2½-inch deep x 6 inch diameter ceramic dish used as a bulb planter (this one has no drainage, so I watered sparingly)

2½-inch deep x 13-inch long x 9½-inch wide oval tray (wicker with a metal lining)

Eco-technique

Divided arrangements: When the ingredients in your bouquet have different requirements, you can devise a two-sectioned vessel. Here, the bulbs needed a small amount of soil, but the cut foliage and branches needed only fresh water. The solution was to place a dish with the planted bulbs in the center of the wicker tray. Then, I arranged the ingredients needing water around its edges, making sure to keep the water level lower than the rim of the center dish.

THE ALLURE OF AMARYLLIS

AS PRECIOUS TO GARDENERS as an enameled Fabergé egg is to collectors, the softball-sized amaryllis bulb can be pricey ($8 to $15 each). But when I compare that to the cost of a floral bouquet, it's easy to persuade myself to buy lots and lots of them at the holidays.

As with paper whites, amaryllis bulbs are magically inclined to bloom indoors. Good quality potting soil, the warmth of a south-facing window, and an occasional drink of water contribute to a growing environment that produces gorgeous, dramatic, lily-like blooms.

I planted two amaryllis bulbs in a glass serving bowl, making sure the necks and shoulders emerged above the soil's surface. Ivory, silver and gold vintage ornaments add some sparkle at the top of the display. Because my vessel doesn't have drainage, I took care to only lightly water the bulbs as they grew. The resulting display graced my dining room for much of December and January, looking quite festive against the lime green walls.

Ingredients:

2 amaryllis bulbs (*Hippeastrum* 'Joker'),
available via mail order, online and garden
centers beginning in autumn. Store in a dry,
cool space until planting. Can be planted and
"forced" four to six weeks prior to desired
bloom.

Vase:

8-inch tall x 8-inch diameter glass trifle dish
used as a bulb planter

Design 101

Better than a flower pot: I realize it's a little unconventional to fill a clear glass trifle dish with soil. But the elegant footed serving piece seems fitting for the graceful amaryllis plants it holds. Glass and ceramic serving pieces can quickly change the ordinary flowering bulb into a stylish floral display. I snagged this piece for $14 at a holiday flea market – and as a bonus, it was actually filled with the slightly faded Christmas balls!

FROSTY WHITE

BY THE TIME THE NEW YEAR ARRIVES, we're all a little tired of evergreen boughs and berry sprays, right? That was my thinking when I conjured a metallic, pewter-toned bouquet, which seems fitting for the first week of the year. I was inspired to design a textural, monochromatic arrangement around the interesting pussy willows grown by my flower farmer-friend Janet Foss.

When I asked her about this unique, multi-branched form, Janet told me she grew it from an unidentified cutting given to her by a customer. The stems are way more attractive than typical ramrod-straight pussy willow branches found at this time of the year.

To begin the arrangement, I cut several pussy willow stems at varying lengths. Once in place, they created a framework that accommodated the softer elements, including two silvery forms of Dusty Miller foliage – one is lacy and the other is broad. And finally, I added a few sprigs of feathery Artemisia from my garden. As a container, this ginger jar's playful, circular pattern and lavender-gray hue complement the botanicals. Even when there's no snow outdoors, this frosty bouquet reminds me of my New England childhood - and the winter-white palette of the season.

Ingredients:

5 branches pussy willow *(Salix caprea)*,
grown by J. Foss Garden Flowers

7 stems each of two forms of Dusty
Miller *(Centaurea cineraria)*, grown by
Charles Little & Co.

7 stems *Artemisia absinthium*, harvested
from my garden

Vase:

9½-inch tall x 9-inch diameter ceramic
ginger jar with 3-inch opening

Design 101

The fashionable vase: Choosing the appropriate vessel for an arrangement is like finding the perfect pair of pumps to complement a cocktail dress. There's good, better or best – and a critical eye is required to make just the right choice. When I made this arrangement, I also photographed two alternate versions: in a tall, white ceramic vase (shown above), and a metallic urn with bands of chrome, brass and bronze. The readers of my blog voted and the pure white vase gained the top spot. While I prefer the ginger-jar vase shown here, the exercise taught me the importance of designing what is personally pleasing. Taste is subjective and while the aesthetic of others may influence you, beauty truly is in the eye of the beholder.

WINTER'S MULTI-HUED PALETTE

IT WAS THE SECOND WEEK OF JANUARY. A hometown garden club asked me to discuss the local-flower movement and to demonstrate how to make a winter arrangement. What?! This was a serious test of my newfound embrace of the seasons. Much to my delight, the dreary, wet, chilly Northwest landscape did not disappoint.

I raided the gardens of several friends, who graciously allowed me to clip from their borders, Felco pruners in hand. My ingredients: cabernet-colored oak leaf hydrangea leaves; the glossy, serrated blades of Corsican hellebores; speckled gold-green Japanese aucuba; scented sweet box, with tiny evergreen leaves and miniscule flowers; witch hazel's burgundy-rust flowering branches and an evergreen Japanese honeysuckle, unwound from my friend Lorene's chain link fence.

Lorene, my co-conspirator in all things gardening, also lent me her vintage cream urn.

Lush, vivid and complex in texture, the bouquet is one of my most favorite of the entire year's creations. It proved to me that the garden's gifts are indeed generous (as are my friends).

Ingredients:

Harvested from Jean Zaputil's Seattle garden:

7 stems Corsican hellebores (*Helleborus argutifolius*)
5 stems Japanese aucuba (*Aucuba japonica* 'Variegata')
7 stems sweet box (*Sarcococca confusa*)

Harvested from Lorene Edwards Forkner's Seattle garden:

3 stems oak leaf hydrangea (*Hydrangea quercifolia*)
7 stems witch hazel (*Hamamelis* x *intermedia* 'Jelena')
3 lengths Japanese honeysuckle (*Lonicera
  japonica* 'Aureoreticulata')

Vase:

12-inch tall x 8½-inch diameter vintage cream urn

Eco-technique

Easy-to-use twine: Here's a great idea I learned from Jennie Greene, a Portland designer and partner in the flower shop called Artis + Greene. To anchor a branch, stem or vine in place, use bind wire. Available from craft stores and floral supply outlets, spools of the pliable, twine-wrapped wire come in tan or green (you'll need wire cutters to work with this material). In this arrangement, I allowed the honeysuckle to drape down the side and wrap around the foot of the vase, using a short length of bind wire to secure it. The tie disappears into the foliage but does the trick to keep things in place.

A BLUE BOWL OF BLOOMS

TWO COMPLETELY DIFFERENT FLOWERS – vivacious tulips and intricate witch hazels – combine to wow the eye in this arrangement, which also makes the most of the color wheel's perfect complementary companions, orange and blue.

The vintage cobalt bowl is a useful vessel because its 6½-inch opening can contain an armload of blooms. Its depth is ample enough to handle the taller witch hazel branches without seeming out of proportion.

This design came together easily, thanks to a hidden flower frog that kept two dozen apricot and pinkish-orange tulips in a compact cluster. The tulips completely fill the bowl's opening – and that alone would make a pretty arrangement. But my garden's witch hazel was at its peak, so I clipped several branches and carefully added them between the tulips, anchoring them into the frog.

At this time of the year in most parts of the country, it's a little too early to expect full-blown tulips to appear. However, thanks to Alm Hill Gardens, located near the Washington-British Columbia border, tulip lovers in my area can enjoy these flowers nearly all year. Owners Gretchen Hoyt and Ben Craft use sustainable practices and toasty greenhouses to grow tulips and other flowering bulbs through the winter months and beyond. They are a fixture at Seattle's Pike Place Market and at many neighborhood farmers' markets – enticing customers with their paint box-like array of fresh, local and luscious flowers.

Ingredients:
    2 dozen mixed spring tulips, grown by Alm Hill Gardens
    7 branches witch hazel (*Hamamelis* x *intermedia* 'Jelena'), harvested from my garden

Vase:
    5-inch tall x 9-inch wide cobalt blue vintage bowl with 6½-inch opening

From the Farmer

Direct from the source: When you shop for flowers at the farmers' market, be sure to ask questions about where and how the flowers you purchase were raised. There is nothing better than meeting the farmer who actually grew your bouquet. You never know when that connection will lead to an invitation to visit a local flower farm!

A NEST FOR MY ORCHIDS

THERE IT WAS, EARLY FEBRUARY, and the floral selection was narrower than during other times of the year. Yet I wasn't without design inspiration, coming from two unexpected sources: colorful twig dogwood branches and cymbidium orchids.

At the Growers' Market, the array of colorful, bundled branches wowed me – their bark revealing warm, rustic hues of gold, cinnamon, coral and burgundy. These twigs enliven any winter arrangement and are long-lasting assets for the floral designer who may otherwise feel limited.

I cut the branches with my sharp pruners, making lots of chopstick-sized lengths. As I filled the two vases, I angled the twigs, alternating right and left sides. As a result, the thin branches formed a modern basket-weave within the clean geometry of the square and rectangle vases.

These twig nests were ideal for resting one or two cymbidiums. The orchids' unusual pale terracotta petals echo the hues of the twigs in which they lie. A classic indoor plant, each cymbidium stem holds several blooms – the antidote to a dreary winter day.

Ingredients:
20-30 cut stems colored twig dogwood (*Cornus sericea*), grown by Oregon Coastal Flowers
1 spray *Cymbidium* Sleeping Dream 'Castle', grown by Peterkort Roses

Vase:
7-inch tall x 4-inch square clear glass vase
4-inch tall x 5-inch long x 3-inch wide clear glass vase

From the Farmer

Orchids as cut flowers: According to Sandra Peterkort Laubenthal, whose family grows roses, lilies and orchids in greenhouses outside of Portland, Oregon, cymbidiums can be displayed as a flower-studded stem or cut individually off the stem for floating or inserting in floral tubes. It's hard to know, however, how fresh the flower is. "What makes the most difference is if they are cut right after blooming," Sandra says. "Look at the lip to see if it has turned pink or is otherwise discolored. This is an indication that the flower has been pollinated by an insect – and that dramatically shortens the cymbidium's lifespan."

CALLAS AND CHERRY BRANCHES

THESE LARGE, OLD-FASHIONED WHITE CALLA LILIES are produced in Oregon from February through June by Patrick and Monika Zweifel of Oregon Coastal Flowers in Tillamook. According to Patrick, callas date back to the time of the Romans, and are today considered one of America's top bridal flowers.

As soon as the first callas of the year began appearing at the Zweifels' flower stall, I was besotted with the elegant form and the way the green stem color bleeds into the base of the white flower, ombré-like. When cut, the standard calla lily measures between 14 and 26 inches tall. The "premium" grade blooms, which I selected for this 20-inch-tall vase, grow to 34 inches tall. Fully opened, the calla flowers span three inches and last for seven to 10 days in water.

I paired the callas with another fabulous Oregon crop, flowering cherry branches. You can just see the green sheath of each pearl-sized bud beginning to open, revealing its pure white flower inside. When brought indoors and placed in room-temperature water, the branches will begin to bloom, changing the way this bouquet looks from one day to the next.

Ingredients:

9 stems white calla lilies (*Zantedeschia aethiopica*), grown by Oregon Coastal Flowers

6 branches white flowering cherry (*Prunus* sp.), harvested by Oregon Coastal Flowers

Vase:

20-inch tall x 7-inch long x 5-inch wide clear glass vase

Place a layer of pebbles in the bottom of this vase to give it visual weight

From the Farmer

Calla curve: When cut, your callas may have a tendency to curve. Patrick Zweifel says this is normal and can be minimized by storing the cut flowers (heads down) in a box overnight. Also, once they are cut and placed in a vase, leave the curved flowers toward the container's outside rim. The callas will naturally straighten up toward the center.

A DISPLAY OF DAFFODILS

CALLED 'KING ALFRED', these vivid yellow, trumpet-shaped daffodils are ever-present in my spring garden. I know they are larger and more garish than others in the Narcissus family, but I do love the confident (shall we say "royal"?) attitude that infuses the garden border or the vase when His Highness shows up.

It's easy to turn any clutch of daffs into an uplifting, cold-weather arrangement. I began this bouquet with branches: the black pussy willow *(Salix gracilistyla* 'Melanostachys'), which produces dark red stems and fuzzy, purple-black catkins.

Arranged symmetrically in the upright vase, the branches provide this bouquet's internal structure. Next, I added maidenhair fern fronds, tucking their thread-thin, stiff black stems between each crossed pussy willow branch.

Then…the daffodils, cut so their flowers emerge just above the twig-and-frond composition. Together, these three elements – flower, foliage and branch – create a simple, interesting design that says: Spring is Almost Here!

Ingredients:
15 stems black pussy willow *(Salix gracilistyla* 'Melanostachys'), grown by Charles Little & Co.
12 stems 'King Alfred' daffodils *(Narcissus* 'King Alfred'), cut from my garden
7 stems maidenhair fern *(Adiantum capillus-veneris)*, grown by Peterkort Roses

Vase:
8-inch tall x 6½-inch diameter green-tinted glass vase

Eco-technique

Timing is everything: I love all three ingredients in this charming arrangement, but there is one drawback to mixing and matching them. The pussy willows gave me two full weeks of enjoyment; the daffodils looked great for a full seven days; and the maidenhair fern began to dry out after just a few days. Maidenhair ferns hail from tropical rain forests, meaning they prefer warm, damp, shaded conditions. Our homes are too dry for their liking. The best way to extend the life of a maidenhair fern (as a cut ingredient or as a house plant) is to keep it out of sunlight, away from a heat source and frequently misted with water.

AMERICAN-GROWN ROSES FOR VALENTINE'S DAY

WHAT DOES THE SUPER BOWL have to do with Valentine's Day? As far as I can tell from watching Super Bowl commercials in recent years, it is Men and Roses. I feel sorry for the unlucky husbands and boyfriends who spend hours in their recliners trying to enjoy what is arguably the biggest professional sports event of the year, while also being assaulted by endless rose commercials. The dial-a-florist rose marketers suggest that true love can only be attained if members of the male species order one (or more) dozen, perfectly red, long-stemmed roses to send their sweetheart for Valentine's Day.

But sadly, those roses are imported … from a very long distance. They were most likely grown on a South American flower farm.

What if the fans of America's biggest sport were instead told about American-grown roses? I am hopeful that enlightened rose-givers hear this news. Since we associate February 14th and romance with roses, it's nice to know there are some wonderful domestic rose sources from greenhouses and fields in Oregon and California. So yes, even in February, when our gardens are unlikely to produce roses, we can ask our florist to order American-grown ones.

My arrangement features three types of gorgeous roses, which I've paired with sprigs of rosemary from my garden and delicate hips. It may not be that 36-inch-long box of imported roses with over-large flower heads and thick, rigid stems, but my bouquet is sweeter, more feminine, lightly fragrant – and it has a home-grown story to tell. It is possible to send eco-conscious love (in the form of American roses).

Ingredients:

All roses grown by Peterkort
Roses of Hillsboro, Oregon:

12 stems 'Prestige' red roses

9 stems 'Black Baccara'
burgundy roses

9 stems 'Gracia' pink spray
roses

20 stems evergreen rosemary
(*Rosmarinus officinalus*),
harvested from my garden

9 stems multiflora rosehips
(*Rosa multiflora*), which
is considered invasive
in many eastern states
(substitute any rose hips
from your garden or local
growers)

Vase:

8-inch tall x 8-inch square with metal cage-style "frog"

From the Farmer

Smaller is better: When it comes to floral design, time and again, I hear from designers who adore domestic hybrid tea roses and spray roses. No, these blooms are not the size of softballs, bred to perfection so they can be shipped like durable produce. The flowers of American-grown hybrid teas are approximately 2 inches in size, slightly fluted and vase-shaped. Some domestic growers are raising German-bred hybrid tea varieties with many extra petals, which make me think of a smaller version of an old English rose. And the spray roses are tiny and quite perfect, with lots of flowers on one branch.

LILIES, TWO WAYS

DEPENDING ON THE CLIMATE where you live, you may conclude that the garden doesn't have much to offer during the chilly months of the year. I disagree. Our choices may be fewer, but winter isn't all about bare twigs and conifer boughs. Case in point: my sweet combination here, featuring the blooms of an early-season flowering shrub and hothouse lilies.

Embellished with a leaf pattern, my antique majolica cachepot called for a voluptuous display of flowers. Neither the vessel nor my eyes were deprived of beauty, thanks to drooping white clusters from a lily-of-the-valley shrub *(Pieris japonica)*. The abundance of flowering branches completely fills the pot's wide opening, creating a nice "base" of soft texture. I love how the pendulous blooms drape over the edge of the green-and-rhubarb-red pot.

For the next ingredient, I couldn't resist choosing white Asiatic lilies. Greenhouse-grown here in the Pacific Northwest, each sturdy stem bears at least five plump buds. I stripped away most of the green foliage and left the stems longer, so the flowers hover above the lily-of-the-valley clusters. And, using restraint, I stopped there. One more type of flower or leaf would only clutter up such a serene combination of two ingredients with "lily" in their names. This long-lived arrangement graced my dining room side table for nearly 10 days, while the lily buds opened, one at a time.

Ingredients:

12 stems lily-of-the-valley shrub *(Pieris japonica)*, harvested by Oregon Coastal Flowers

5 stems white 'Navona' Asiatic lilies, grown by Peterkort Roses

Vase:

9-inch tall x 9¼-inch diameter majolica cachepot from the late 1800s. I found this unique piece in Palm Springs, in a shop otherwise filled with 1950s art glass. I simply couldn't resist the botanical charm of the piece, so I splurged and ended up flying home with it on my lap!

Eco-technique

Flower frogs: I've made it a personal goal to stabilize flower stems with organic methods rather than the conventional florist's foam or "Oasis." That product, I have learned, contains formaldehyde and does not break down in landfills. An old-fashioned flower frog (in ceramic, glass or metal) is a great alternative. You can find flower frogs at flea markets or tag sales for a few dollars (or raid your grandmother's supply). One of my favorites is a half-dome cage. It sinks to the bottom of the container and has ¾-inch square openings, ideal for woody stems. This is an arranging tool of the past, seriously useful for the present-day!

JUST ADD LIME

THE SPRING GREEN COLOR OF NEW GROWTH is indescribably beautiful. I notice it suddenly, almost as if our first slightly warm day of the year flips a hidden switch inside deciduous trees and shrubs, mature evergreens and returning perennials. There's a youthful glow to the earth and a shimmer of pale citron hovers over every growing thing.

Capturing that lemon-lime spectrum in a vase began with the best source of the color: the *Euphorbia*. Commonly called spurge, this Mediterranean perennial produces fantastic green-on-green texture. What looks like a flower is actually the "cyathium," a cup-like bract that's almost neon green. The short, fleshy stems of donkey tail spurge and the nodding heads of *Euphorbia characias* look perfect when added to a crackled-lime ceramic vase (see sidebar for tips on preparing euphorbia for arrangements).

A little contrast comes from variegated geranium, clipped from a potted plant that spent winter under a grow light in my garage. I topped off the intense lime with lemon-colored garden elements: forsythia branches and a variety of daffodils. These stems stay upright through the thicket of lime foliage. It's a happy place to be.

Ingredients:

All ingredients were harvested
from my Seattle garden:

5 stems donkey tail spurge
(Euphorbia myrsinites)

3 stems *Euphorbia characias*

5 stems variegated rose
mint scented geranium
(Pelargonium Graveolens
Group 'Variegata')

7 stems forsythia branches
(Forsythia x intermedia)

7 stems daffodils (Narcissus sp.),
unknown cultivars

Vase:

5¾-inch tall x 5-inch diameter
glazed ceramic vase

From the Farmer

Working with euphorbia: Most plants in the spurge family produce a milky-white substance when cut. It can be irritating to the skin, so be sure to wear gloves when handling the plant. While harvesting, I place the stems in a bucket of water, separating them from any other cut ingredients. Then I bring them into my kitchen where I dunk the tip of each euphorbia stem into a bowl filled with boiling water from the teakettle. This seals the stems. Some experts recommend searing the tips in a stovetop flame, but that has proven too messy for my liking.

HEADY HYACINTH

A SINGULAR SENSATION – for the eye as well as the nose – hyacinths are so stunning that it's hard to justify pairing them with any other flower. In fact, you really only need one hyacinth bulb, cupped in a special forcing glass, to experience the arrival of spring on your windowsill.

Gretchen Hoyt and Ben Craft grew these pink, lavender and indigo hybrid hyacinths at Alm Hill Gardens. When I brought home the mixed bunch from the farmers' market, they filled my car with a heady perfume – a bonus! I tore open the brown Kraft paper and noticed two things: First, the stems were extra-long, nearly 10 inches; second, the bulbs were still attached to the bottom of each flower. These hyacinths were far superior to anything I could grow in my own garden.

To arrange them, I opted for a simple European-style bouquet. I wrapped linen twine around the gathered stems and foliage, tied a bow, and placed the spiraled bunch in a glass vase. Seeing the twine through the glass adds a touch of whimsy to this effortless bouquet.

Ingredients:
8 stems hyacinths (*Hyacinthus orientalis*), grown by Alm Hill Gardens

Vase:
7-inch tall x 7-inch square glass cube

Seasonal Choices

About those long stems: The typical garden hyacinth blooms on a relatively short stem – maybe 4-5 inches at the most. This limits the way hyacinths can be used in floral arrangements. According to Gretchen Hoyt, the way to stretch those stems is to trick them into wanting more light. "The longer you can deny them light, the more they stretch," she explains. At the commercial flower farm, this process begins in dark coolers where bulbs are pre-chilled. When they are transferred to the greenhouse, the hyacinth crates are placed (in the shadows) beneath tables where tulips grow. If Gretchen wants to elongate those stems even further, "I'll throw newspaper over them," she says. Leaving bulbs on the stems is optional, but some designers do so to give the arrangement a rustic appearance.

MAGNOLIAS AND MORE

OUR NEIGHBORS KIM AND JAKE have a stunning *Magnolia grandiflora* that we view from our sitting room. A perfect landscape tree, it's evergreen, with glossy, leathery leaves that measure nine inches long. The underside of each leaf is slightly fuzzy and rusty-brown, especially enticing in arrangements when companion ingredients are chosen to accentuate their color and texture.

Permission received to clip a few stems, I started this arrangement with sprays of magnolia foliage. Depending on how each stem fell, either the shiny green surface or the matte-rust area of the leaves revealed themselves. Next, I added apricot-orange parrot tulips, with slightly darker margins on each petal's edge. I like how the tulips drape casually between the magnolia leaves, their color echoing the rusty-brown.

The upright elements include: seasonal branches of rosemary, deciduous magnolia with tight, velvety buds, and unusual, cinnamon-red Japanese fantail willows (*Salix udensis* 'Sekka'). Together, this bouquet is as bold and eye-catching as the magnolia tree I love to admire.

Ingredients:

5 stems southern magnolia
(*Magnolia grandiflora*), harvested
from my neighbors' garden

12 stems apricot-hued parrot tulips,
grown by Alm Hill Gardens

5 stems evergreen rosemary
(*Rosmarinus officinalis*), harvested
from my garden

3 stems Japanese fantail willow
(*Salix udensis* 'Sekka'), grown by
J. Foss Garden Flowers

3 stems deciduous magnolia in bud,
harvested by Oregon Coastal
Flowers

Vase:

17-inch tall x 7-inch diameter cream
urn

Design 101

Proportion and Scale: These two related principles are among the most challenging to pull off correctly
– in interiors and garden design, as well as in a vase. Proportion usually refers to size relationships within a
composition, such as how each of the botanicals in this tall vessel is visually powerful. There are no wispy
ingredients and the height of the arrangement is equal to the height of the vase. Scale indicates size in
comparison to some constant, such as the human body. That's where the terms "small scale" or "large scale"
come in, since they refer to the out-of-the-ordinary size of things. With that in mind, think about the ideal interior
setting for this vase. I think it would look stunning as the welcoming urn in a grand foyer or at the center of a
large buffet table.

DOING IT YOURSELF, WITH STYLE

❦

Floral techniques, aesthetics, care, resources/supplies

The practice is timeless. The gesture is universal. Inspired by the exquisite beauty of a garden or by the sentiment of a special occasion, we gather flowers and foliage and place them in a vessel to display in our homes or give to another. Floral design is a three-dimensional art form that blends horticulture and nature with sculptural composition. At its best, bouquet making is a personal expression unique to the designer's tastes and point of view.

Behind the artistry there are some practicalities: tools, supplies and techniques; an understanding of when plants grow and bloom; an appreciation of color theory and the principles of design. The more frequently you arrange flowers, the more familiar you'll become with each of these aspects – and many are covered in the following pages.

I feel rewarded by the results of my "slow flowers" odyssey. I embarked on a 52-week exploration of design, during seasons both abundant and spare, relying on locally-grown elements from my garden, nearby farms and flower fields. Never was I disappointed by what I discovered and learned.

I encourage you to give it a try and take your own creative journey.

EARTH-FRIENDLY FLORAL TECHNIQUES

I prefer taking a "green" approach to my bouquet-making, using several methods that pre-date the introduction of florist's foam. So may designers have told me over the years that they wish the floral industry could come up with a product that stabilizes stems in an arrangement, but that's non-toxic and healthy to handle. Many of the dark green foam products currently sold to florists are formaldehyde-based. They do not break down in landfills and designers who regularly work with the material experience skin rashes or other symptoms.

Yes, it's tricky to get flower and foliage stems to tilt just the right way or make an arrangement look full and lush without using florist's foam, but I am quite satisfied with the ecologically-friendly alternatives covered here. They're worth rediscovering.

Twigs

Twigs and branches are decorative elements that can be inserted in a vase first, before other components are added. They help stabilize flowers and foliage and become part of the finished composition.

Select branches that complement your design and can serve as the framework that supports the other ingredients. Here, black pussy willow *(Salix gracilistyla* 'Melanostachys') is arranged so the stems tilt outward, overlapping one another at the bottom of the vase. Next, add foliage, such as maidenhair fern fronds, tucked between the crossed willow twigs. Finally, insert flowers, such as trumpet-shaped daffodils that emerge just above the twig-and-frond composition.

Chicken Wire

Available by the roll (in various widths) from hardware and home improvement stores, chicken wire is pliable, lightweight and affordable. Trim it to the desired length with wire cutters. Wear gloves to protect your hands, especially while shaping the wire into a mushroom-cap form.

Once a length of chicken wire is cut and formed, place it into the container. Allow the domed shape of the wire to emerge above the vase's rim – this ensures a fuller look. Next, insert a layer of foliage, making sure it drapes over the edges of the container and hides the chicken wire. Then add other short and tall ingredients. Here, I used oak leaf hydrangea *(Hydrangea quercifolia)* leaves, branches of purple beautyberry *(Callicarpa bodinieri* 'Profusion'), red rose hips, purple coneflower seed heads *(Echinacea* sp.) and pincushion flowers *(Scabiosa stellata)*. Pale lime 'Supergreen' roses, cut short to nestle into the composition, add a touch of elegance.

Flower Frogs

I love old-fashioned metal, ceramic or glass flower frogs. These floral design accessories offer today's flower lovers an eco-friendly way to create bouquets without florist's foam. See pages 135-136 for places to source vintage and new flower frogs.

Place a vintage metal frog in the bottom of the vase (this one measures 2¾-inches tall x 5¼-inches in diameter). Some designers prefer to anchor the frog with sticky floral clay. Fill the vase with stems of lily-of-the-valley shrub

(Pieris japonica), allowing its drooping clusters to cascade over the rim. Insert Asiatic lilies. The flowers will stay upright and perfectly positioned, stabilized by the flower frog and the Pieris stems.

Other Techniques

Excelsior, also known as aspenwood, is a shredded wood fiber that wineries use as packing material for bottles. Pull the tangles apart to loosen before placing in a vase; add water. Insert stems into the mass of fibers. The fibers will hold stems and branches in place. If you use a clear vessel, they become part of the design. And when the arrangement is finished, the fibers can be tossed into the compost bin along with everything else. (I learned this easy technique from Melissa Feveyear, of Terra Bella Flowers in Seattle.)

Pebbles can be both decorative and functional. Available at garden centers and craft stores by the bag, tumbled rocks come in several sizes. Their effectiveness depends on how many you place in the bottom of a vase. If you use a shallow layer, only the tips of flower stems will poke into the bed of pebbles. If you use a deeper layer, the material does a better job of stabilizing stems, although your vase will be heavy to transport. After use, be sure to thoroughly clean and wash the pebbles, to reduce bacteria.

Hand-tied bouquets are first arranged while holding stems in your hand. When completed, you should be able to re-cut them and drop the entire arrangement into a vase, where everything stays in place. The stems can also be wrapped and secured with floral tape, then finished with decorative fabric ribbon. Special thanks to floral artist Nicole Cordier of the Seattle Wholesale Growers Market for demonstrating the steps as shown in the photographs on the opposite page.

1. Assemble and prepare all of the elements (strip off excess foliage).

2. Gather a cluster of flowers in your left hand. Here, three sunflowers form a triangle-shaped arrangement.

3. Add a grouping of the second element, tucking each stem between the original flowers. Rotate bouquet in your hand to distribute the new elements evenly.

4. Working from the top, place accent flowers between the first and second flower heads. Thread several new flower stems from the top of the bouquet; then reach underneath and pull the cut ends until the flowers are where you want them to be.

5. Add foliage. Create a "collar" to surround the base of the bouquet or, as is demonstrated here, integrate the foliage with the existing flowers. Add their stems from the top of the arrangement (as in Step 4) and use your free hand to position them for desired placement.

6. While holding the entire bouquet in one hand, cut all the stems to an even length. Place finished bouquet in vase. The floral elements will stay in place because the stems have knit themselves together while you rotated the bouquet.

7. Final bouquet includes sunflowers *(Helianthus annuus* 'Sunrich Gold'), flowering kale *(Brassica oleracea),* pincushion flower *(Scabiosa atropurpurea* 'Black Knight') and *Eucalyptus gunnii.*

A BOTANICAL RAINBOW

R-O-Y-G-B-I-V. Do you remember learning about rainbows and prisms in elementary school?

Red-Orange-Yellow-Green-Blue-Indigo-Violet: the seven bands of the rainbow; the result of rain + sun in the sky.

These hues are represented by both the artist's color wheel and nature's flora. You can see the incredible diversity of flowers and foliage depicted here as a floral designer's color wheel.

Nicole Cordier, a gifted artist and manager at the Seattle Wholesale Growers Market, created six of these beautiful arrangements for an industry event. I was smitten by her designs and asked to photograph them for *Slow Flowers* (the elements were grown in and harvested from Northwest fields within a few hours' drive of where we are based in Seattle).

Taking a little liberty with the original color wheel, Nicole's bouquets represent Red, Orange, Yellow, Green, Blue and Pink flowers. Later, I asked her to add White and Black bouquets to complete this color spectrum. "Black" is relative – you can see that most of the ingredients are deep maroon-plum in hue, but you get the idea.

I find these arrangements quite inspiring. They capture my imagination with the possibilities of working with color – and I hope they will do the same for you.

And forget about color "rules." They are only guidelines, worth breaking. Harold Piercy, principal of the Constance Spry Flower School in England, wrote in 1983: "…in flower arrangement, I have always found it advisable to discard any preconceptions about colours." He went on to write: "Keep an open mind and do not be ruled by the colour wheel. You may hit upon unexpected satisfactory results during your experiments."

Glossary of color terms

Primary: These pure colors include Red, Yellow and Blue

Secondary: Combinations of two primary colors, including Orange (Red + Yellow), Green (Blue + Yellow) and Purple (Red + Blue)

Tertiary: A combination of one primary color and one secondary color

Complementary/Contrasting: Color "pairs" that reside opposite each other on the color wheel

Analogous: Adjacent colors on the color wheel, related to a dominant primary hue

Monochromatic: A single hue, or variations of one color, including tints, shades and tones

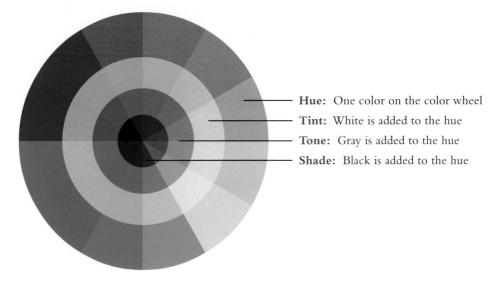

Hue: One color on the color wheel

Tint: White is added to the hue

Tone: Gray is added to the hue

Shade: Black is added to the hue

HARVESTING AND POST-HARVEST CARE

Gathering fresh flowers from your garden and bringing them into your home is a source of great joy. The next best thing to growing floral ingredients yourself is to source them from other growers. Here are some of the techniques learned from my own flower harvesting, as well as advice from savvy flower farmers:

- ❧ Cut flowers early in the morning or late in the day when the weather is cooler. In my area, I prefer to cut in the evening when the dew has dried from the flower heads and foliage.

- ❧ In most cases, you can select and cut flowers that are about half opened, ensuring that they will continue to "bloom" in the vase. Look for a little bit of the bloom color emerging from the bud. Some flowers, like dahlias, will not continue to open after being cut. You should experiment with one or two flowers before harvesting a major section of the garden.

- ❧ Use clean, sharp floral shears or pruners. Place cut flowers, leaf stems and branches into water immediately (making sure the bucket has first been scrubbed clean to slow the growth of bacteria).

- ❧ Once you bring flowers indoors, work in a cool, dry space. I like to work in my garage for these reasons: Even in the summer, it's like a walk-in cooler. Plus, it's close to the compost bin.

- ❧ Strip or cut the foliage from stems, paying particular attention to the portion that will be under water (it's nice to leave a few leaves close to the flower heads). Re-cut stems at a 45-degree angle, using a clean, sharp knife or shears. Place flowers up to their necks in room-temperature water until you are ready to arrange.

RESOURCES AND SUPPLIES

VASES

Unless noted, the vintage vases are from my private collection.

p. 22-23:

Decor Bon Bon Footed Square Bowl, Rosanna Inc.
http://www.rosannainc.com/bowls/
decor-bon-bon-footed-square-bowl/

p. 24-25; 116-117:

Roost Recycled Glass Wall Terrarium,
aHa! Modern Living
http://www.ahamodernliving.com/store/pc/
Roost-Recycled-Glass-Wall-Terrarium-
7p385.htm

Roost Flower Frog and Glass Vase,
aHa! Modern Living
http://www.ahamodernliving.com/store/pc/
Roost-Flower-Frogs-Glass-Vases-7p368.htm

p. 28-29; 104-105:

Glazed blue vase and pale lavender ginger jar,
Capers Home
http://caperscapers.blogspot.com/

p. 40-41; 50-51:

Crackle-glaze vase, various sizes, Ravenna Gardens
www.ravennagardens.com

p. 62-64:

Yellow-glazed fluted vase,
Frances Palmer's Pearl Collection
http://www.francespalmerpottery.com/

p. 72-73:

Antique-finished urn with handles,
Floral Supply Syndicate
http://www.francespalmerpottery.com/

p. 74-75:

Licorice Stick Vase,
Tracy Glover Objects and Lighting
http://www.tracygloverstudio.com/

p. 88-89:

Tabletop Cast-iron Centerpiece Urn,
A Rustic Garden
http://www.arusticgarden.com/5cairtatopce.html

FLOWERS

In addition to plants that I grow (and those shared by friends), here is an alphabetical listing of the flower farmers who supplied and inspired me.

Alm Hill Gardens; www.growingwashington.org
Charles Little & Co.; charleslittle@comcast.net
Choice Bulb Farms, 360-424-4685;
www.choicebulb.com
Dan's Dahlias, 360-482-2406; www.dansdahlias.com
Echo Lake Peonies, 907-262-5408;
www.echolakefarm.com
Everyday Flowers; everydayflowers@live.com
J. Foss Garden Flowers; www.jfossgardenflowers.com
Jello Mold Farm, 206-290-3154;
www.jellomoldfarm.com
Lila B. Flowers, Gardens and Events, 415-563-6681;
www.lilabdesign.com
Marigold and Mint, 206-682-3111;
www.marigoldandmint.com
Midnight Sun Peonies, 907-260-4183;
www.midnightsunpeonies.com
Northern Pacific Farm, 503-266-8479;
www.northernpacificfarm.com
Ojeda Farms; ojedafarms@hotmail.com

Oregon Coastal Flowers, 888-815-0885;
www.flowersbulbs.com

Peterkort Roses, 503-628-1005;
www.peterkortroses.com

Repetto's Greenhouse Florist, 650-726-6414;
www.repettosgreenhouseflorist.com

Succulent Gardens, 831-632-0482;
www.sgplants.com

Sunshine Crafts and Flowers, 509-332-2306;
sunshinecraftsandflowers@gmail.com

Westmont Park Roses, 509-398-ROSE;
martinjohnr13@gmail.com

Other resources for American-grown cut flowers:

Association of Specialty Cut Flower Growers,
440-774-2887; www.ascfg.org

California Cut Flower Commission,
916-441-1701; www.ccfc.org

Growing for Market, 800-307-8949;
www.growingformarket.com

Seattle Wholesale Growers Market, 206-838-1523;
www.seattlewholesalegrowersmarket.com

TOOLS

Arranged for You: VaseBrace for transporting vases,
www.arrangingsupplies.com

Corona Clippers: Floral Shears with 2¼-inch blades
(FS 4200), www.coronatoolusa.com

Fiskars: Comfort Grip(R) Floral Snips (96386935J),
www.fiskars.com

Wildflower Seed & Tool Co.: Rose Thorn Stripper,
www.wildflower-seed.com

FLOWER FROGS

Find vintage glass, ceramic or metal flower frogs at flea markets, thrift stores or yard sales. Good online sources include eBay.com and Etsy.com.

Easy Arranger is a bloom-shaped wire grid that fits over the mouth of a vase; it can be adapted to various widths; www.easyarranger.com

Kenzan, also called pin holder or needle holder, is an Ikebana tool that works with many types of flowers; www.stonelantern.com

Perfect Arranger is a stainless-steel wire mesh cylinder for arranging flowers and stems; www.cedarlakegardengoods.com

CUT FLOWER AND FOLIAGE INDEX

Note: *Botanical names are listed in Italics. Where both the common and botanical name are the same, I have only included botanical names. USDA Zones follow each plant name.*

References:

American Horticultural Society A-Z Encyclopedia of Garden Plants (DK; 2004)

Flora: A Gardener's Encyclopedia (Timber Press, 2003)

ABOUT THE AUTHOR

Debra Prinzing is a Seattle- and Los Angeles-based outdoor living expert who writes and lectures on gardens and home design. She has a background in textiles, journalism, landscape design and horticulture. A frequent speaker for botanical garden, horticultural society and flower show audiences, Debra is also a regular radio and television guest. Her six books include *The 50 Mile Bouquet* (St. Lynn's Press, 2012), Garden Writers Association Gold Award–winning *Stylish Sheds and Elegant Hideaways* (Clarkson-Potter/Random House, 2008) and *The Abundant Garden* (Cool Springs Press/ Thomas Nelson, 2005). She is particularly thrilled that *Slow Flowers* is her first book to include not only her writing but her design and photography work.

Debra is a contributing garden editor for *Better Homes & Gardens* and her feature stories on architecture and design appear regularly in the Saturday/Home section of the *Los Angeles Times.* She also contributes to *Country Gardens, GRAY* magazine, *Garden Design, Organic Gardening, Horticulture, Fine Gardening, Landscape Architecture, Sunset, Alaska Airlines Magazine, flower* magazine, *Romantic Homes* and others. Debra serves as president of the Garden Writers Association, as a board member of the Seattle Wholesale Growers Market, and she was co-founder of Greatgardenspeakers.com.

Learn more at: **www.debraprinzing.com**.

my early flower seed-planting efforts

ACKNOWLEDGMENTS

I learned so many lessons while creating this book, but the most important one is: It takes a village to make a bouquet. So here is my bouquet of heartfelt thanks to those who made my year of *Slow Flowers* a great one:

My dear family, including husband Bruce Brooks and sons Alex Brooks and Benjamin Brooks. Their encouragement, love and sense of humor are as essential to me as oxygen. My wonderful parents, Anita and Fred Prinzing, who shopped for vintage flower frogs, gifted me family heirloom vases, and faithfully asked: "How is the book coming along?"

My friends who shared everything from vessels to garden clippings, including Jean Zaputil, Lorene Edwards Forkner, Ellen Spector-Platt, Charlotte Behnke, Jayme Jenkins, Cristi Walden, Susan Harkavy and Tracy Glover. Jean, Lorene and Gillian Mathews were always game for vintage flea market excursions – where I found many of my vases, flower frogs and photo props.

The flower farmers who so generously answered my questions and shared advice, tips and samples. You'll find all their names and contact information on pages 135-136. I owe special thanks to Diane Szukovathy, co-owner of Jello Mold Farm, who served as horticultural editor and advisor on post-harvesting practices. She stepped in at an essential time, a true champion for this project. Dr. Pat Holloway of the University of Alaska at Fairbanks and Beth VanSandt and Kurt Weichhand of Scenic Place Peonies graciously hosted me during my Alaska peony tour; many others who are part of the Alaska Peony Growers Association (www.alaskapeonies.org) made sure that my trip unforgettable. The California Cut Flower Commission, including CEO/Ambassador Kasey Cronquist and many of his board, as well as Janice Wills Curtis and Kathleen Williford, always say "yes" to my requests for help; they have supported my California appearances with donations of gorgeous Cali-grown blooms. The Seattle Wholesale Growers Market family, including the ever-inspiring Beverly Burrows, and my weekly pals, Kim Millikin and Nicole Cordier, literally made sure I had the seasonal flowers, leaves, branches, grasses and stems that made this book possible. I'm honored to have joined the board of that dynamic, pioneering flower-farming cooperative.

So many have supported my lectures and floral design demonstrations, including Janet Endsley of the Northwest Flower & Garden Show; Julie Chai and Kathleen Brenzel of *Sunset* and *Sunset's* Celebration Weekend; Jenny Andrews and Betsy Flack of the Garden Conservancy; and countless garden clubs and horticultural organizations, each of whom has become a strong advocate for the slow flower movement.

In *The 50 Mile Bouquet*, I thanked many of the newspaper and magazine editors who supported my storytelling. But this time, I want to single out James Augustus Baggett of *Country Gardens* magazine. He loves gathering and sharing stories about authentic American gardeners, flower farmers and designers as much as I do!

Wherever I find myself, I seek out flower farmers, thanks to the many contacts and friends I've made through the Association for Specialty Cut Flower Growers. What an amazing group of people who love and grow the flowers that inspire so many designers.

A special thanks to ABC Good Morning America superstar Lara Spencer, who definitely knows her way around a flea market, for lending her words of support for this book. I'm so appreciative that her producers Sabrina Peduto and Kelly Hagan enthusiastically facilitated our long-distance exchanges – they each deserve a big, *local* bouquet! Speaking of bouquets, designer extraordinaire Bess Wyrick of NYC-based Celadon & Celery went way beyond the expected bounds of friendship to create a gorgeous vase filled with summer garden hydrangeas, which she hand-delivered to Lara's office, along with my book information. I don't know how I'll ever show my gratitude for that generous gesture.

Finally, the largest bouquet of all goes to the talented individuals I've worked with on the creation of *Slow Flowers*. First, the St. Lynn's Press team: visionary publisher Paul Kelly, gifted editor Cathy Dees and brilliant art director Holly Rosborough. Willo Bellwood and Bob Meador, now of Metric Media Inc., have worked their magic on my web site since 2004, including the latest facelift – thank you! And finally, Lola Honeybone of MediaWorks Nashville: You are the world's very best book publicist. Since 2005, you have been in my corner and I'm so fortunate that we've teamed up again.

FINAL THOUGHTS

*I'd rather have roses on my table
than diamonds on my neck.*

– Emma Goldman

My obsession with using seasonal, locally grown floral elements might seem quaint to some, but there is a story behind the flowers that I hope resonates with anyone who embraces my Slow Flowers philosophy. I believe we need to treasure and support the American flower farmer. These men and women, their families and employees, are passionate about the beautiful, fragrant, high quality fruits (or shall I say flowers?) of their labor; they work long hours to generate a living and they believe in land stewardship. Most of us can get behind that idea. According to a recent survey conducted by the U.S. Farmers & Ranchers Alliance, 65% of people who drive past a farm feel that they know the farmer. Isn't that amazing? Whether or not we actually meet the individuals who cultivate farmland, we experience a sense of kinship when we see fields and meadows filled with their flowers and food crops.

Certainly, there's nothing more fulfilling than growing flowers in your own backyard. Yet constraints of time or space may leave you with empty vases, heading to the market to purchase something beautiful. I urge you to consider the benefits of choosing local blooms – from their small "flower mile" to the growers' earth-friendly practices. There are some who equate "buy local" marketing campaigns with giving one's business to the hometown flower shop or chain store's floral department. But that's not enough – because unless that flower seller can assure you that the product came from a LOCAL grower, or at the very least an American farm, then sadly, there's a big chance those flowers were imported. Please ask. Join me and vote with your pocketbook. Being intentional with our choices might just save the American flower farm from extinction.